The World According to Foggy

CARL FOGARTY

The World According to Foggy

HEADLINE

First published in 2018
by HEADLINE PUBLISHING GROUP

3

Cataloguing in Publication Data is available from the British Library

Hardback ISBN 978 1 4722 5241 8
Trade paperback ISBN 978 1 4722 5323 1

Typeset in Bliss Light by Jouve (UK), Milton Keynes

Printed and bound in Great Britain by Clays Ltd, St Ives Plc

MIX
Paper from
responsible sources
FSC® C104740

Headline's policy is to use papers that are natural, renewable and recyclable
products and made from wood grown in well-managed forests and other
controlled sources. The logging and manufacturing processes are expected
to conform to the environmental regulations of the country of origin.

To Michaela, my rock;
to Danielle and Claudia, who aggravate the hell
out of me, but I love dearly;
and to all my family and friends, past and present, without
whose crazy tales this book would not be possible.

Contents

CONTENTS

CONTENTS

INTRODUCTION:
STOP! IN THE NAME OF LOVE

Let's kick off in a bar in Barbados – literally. Ragamuffins, in the sleepy village of Holetown, is famous for its Sunday night drag act. We were on holiday with a few friends to celebrate my wife Michaela's 40th birthday in November 2006. You have to book months in advance to get a table on Sunday night and this was planned to be one of the highlights of the trip, although we'd already had a few laughs.

The previous day, we had chartered a fishing boat to try and catch some marlin. All we caught was an eyeful. The local captain was a huge bloke, who looked like he'd been sleeping on his boat for weeks because his clothes were filthy and full of rips. But he was a real character and, after he told us how to use all the equipment, we all settled down to watch our rods. The captain plonked himself on a stool at the front of the boat and started to mend his nets. I was just nodding off when Michaela dug me in the ribs, killing herself laughing but trying to keep quiet at the same time, which is never easy for her.

'Don't turn round quickly but look at what's under the captain's stool,' she giggled.

I could see that I was the last one in on the joke, because the rest of our group were already in hysterics. I swivelled slowly around, and it was impossible to miss. The captain's 'tackle' had poked through one of the many holes in his shorts and was actually touching the deck. Let's just say it would have been useful if we'd had a man overboard. I slowly picked up my phone and tried to take a picture without him noticing, but he spotted me and realised his cock was hanging out, so he scuttled off below deck and came back up in a different pair of shorts, which were still full of holes – but not in a spot where his cock could dangle down. For the record, we all caught tuna – but mine was the biggest.

Ragamuffins is a no-frills place. It's basically a shack built on stilts with no air conditioning and only plantation shutters on the windows for ventilation. We were all sweating like racehorses and I was pleased when they sat me right next to the main door, with my back to the window, where I could see everything that was going on inside. The drag show – three massive Bajan transvestites singing all the usual camp songs like Abba's 'Dancing Queen' – started just when the food started to arrive.

Then in staggers the golfer, Ian Woosnam, who had captained the Ryder Cup team that beat the USA a couple of months earlier. He had a house on Barbados and it looked like he hadn't stopped celebrating since. It took him a moment to get his bearings, then the cheeky bastard grabbed a prawn straight off the plate of Michaela's friend, Tracey. Nobody bothered too much, because we were all enjoying the show. Except for my mate Kevin Moore, who used to play football for Swansea and now runs a nursing home. His two passions in life are motorbikes and golf, so Kev was like a kid in a sweet shop when Woosie was swaying behind his chair.

'Carl, here's my phone, take a picture of me with Woosie in the background,' he shouted across the table.

'Shut up, will you,' I said. 'I'm not taking a picture of him. Leave me alone and let me eat my food.' But Kev wouldn't take no for an answer and kept pestering me to take the pic.

'Oh, for f**k's sake, give me the f**king phone then,' I said, and I stood up to take the shot. The flash went off and Woosie turned around, almost in slow motion. He didn't recognise me, and I think he thought he had been snapped by the paparazzi.

'Get rid of that picture,' he slurred.

'Look, mate, it's obviously not for me. My mate Kev's a massive fan – it's for him,' I shouted, but he couldn't hear me above the noise of the singers.

'Just give me the f**king phone and I'll delete it then,' he snapped and lunged across the table, half-trying to grab it out my hand and half-trying to give me a slap. I instinctively landed one right on his chin. And all hell broke loose. Woosie rocked back and then lunged again but Kev, who is pretty handy in a scrap, wrestled him to the floor and landed on top of him with his knee on his chest and his hands on his throat.

'Calm down, you idiot,' yelled Kev. 'You're a hero of mind, but I'll knock you out if I have to.' Woosie was threatening to tear Kev limb from limb and by now the whole restaurant was watching. A huge bouncer waded in, but Kev managed to get him in a headlock, too.

'Look, I'll let you go,' Kev yelled at the bouncer. 'But I'm trying to calm this guy down. And if you start on me, we're going to have a problem.' The bouncer realised what was going on and managed to bundle Woosie outside so Kev could let him go.

As this was happening, the drag act played on. And I will remember this image until the day I die – my mate Kev with an enormous bouncer in a headlock and a British sporting icon by the throat on the floor, while three transvestites continued to sing 'Stop! In the Name of Love'. I kid you not.

But Woosie was still spitting feathers outside because the bouncer would not let him back in. He was screaming for Kev to continue it outside, but Kev refused to be drawn into a street brawl. All this time I had been pinned in by the table, so I couldn't really help Kev out. And my curried chicken was going cold – it was a shame for it to go to waste. So I finished my meal, which was really good, and then realised that Kev hadn't touched his steak. 'He seems to have his hands full, so he probably won't notice if that goes, too,' I thought. Then I felt a nudge in my back and turned around to find one of the locals pushing a piece of 3 x 2 wood through the shutters, with a big nail stuck through the end.

'Hey, man,' he whispered. 'You might be needing dis if tings turn ugly again.'

'What the f**k? No way, mate, I'm not getting involved in any of that stuff,' I told him, and pushed it back through the slats just when Kev was sitting back down.

'I don't believe this,' he said. 'You don't lift a finger to help me fight *your battle*, you've tooled yourself up – and polished off my steak. Thanks, mate.'

He didn't get any help from my manager, Neil Bramwell, either. I had just launched a new *Hell for Leather* DVD for that Christmas and the fight wasn't over before Neil was planning how some publicity about the fight might be great for sales.

Woosie's wife, Glendryth, later came inside to try and make the peace and recognised me immediately. 'Oh no,' she said. 'Ian will be mortified when he realises it's you!' She went back outside, where a bit of a street party had started up at closing time, and explained everything to her hus-band, who had finally calmed down. When we eventually joined their group outside to laugh it all off, one of his mates told me that Woosie's dad had wanted him to be a boxer, and that he was pretty handy with his fists as a lad. If I had known that, I might not have smacked him in the kipper. As for the bouncer, his pride had obviously been a bit wounded by Kev's headlock.

'Your mate must work out all de time,' he said.

'Not really,' I laughed. 'He just plays a bit of golf now and again. Per-haps you should go to the gym a bit more.'

A lot of people were taking pictures of us together outside Ragamuffins and I was sure something would get into the newspapers. I could see the headlines: 'Foggy Knocks a Golfer Woosie' or perhaps 'Bike Racer Throt-tles Woosnam' . . .

But we didn't hear any more about it until around three or four years later when someone spotted an interview with *Dragon's Den* tycoon,

Duncan Bannatyne, in the holiday section of the *Sunday Times*. When asked about his most unusual holiday moment, he answered: 'Sat in a restaurant in Barbados watching a drag act sing "Stop! In the Name of Love" when a fight broke out between motorbike racer Carl Fogarty and a famous golfer.' Interesting that they named me, but not Woosie. Perhaps a bit of fisticuffs didn't fit with the *Sunday Times'* expectations of golfers, not like us smelly bikers.

None of us had any idea Duncan had been there that night. And my first chance to talk to him about it was when I was in Australia to crown the new King or Queen of the Jungle from *I'm A Celebrity* . . . Duncan was voted off on the day of my first appearance on the ITV2 show and he came straight over to me when it finished.

'The last time I saw you . . .' he started to say.

'I can stop you right there,' I said. 'I know exactly what you are going to say.'

'It's not the kind of thing you see every day,' he laughed.

Well, he doesn't live in the weird and wonderful world of Carl Fogarty . . .

1

IT'S NOT JUST CRICKET

Golf was never one of my favourite sports, long before that slight alter-cation with Woosie. A few people have tried to persuade me to take it up over the years, but I just don't have the patience or ability to concentrate for four hours. I've had a go a couple of times when I've been away racing, but I usually come back with a few less clubs than I started with. And I would rather paint the dog kennel and watch it dry than watch golf on television, although I do look at the famous courses and think it would be great to ride my motocross bike around them. There would be some great berms on the fairways and jumps out of the bunkers. How cool would it be to launch off that bridge on the 18th at St Andrews, do about five big doughnuts on the green and then ride off while the members are waiting to play their shots? That would have to be pretty close to the top of my bucket list, so if any of the committee at St Andrews are reading, just give me a bell!

Golf is quite popular among motorbike racers, especially when there are free days between tests or races abroad. And there are some pretty handy players around. It would be fair to say that my mate and fellow superbike racer, James Whitham, is not one of these. But he was always willing to give it a go and arranged to play with the Scottish rider Brian Morrison the day after the World Superbike race in Indonesia in 1994. I had been leading the first race with a few laps to go when my bike broke down and James went on to win his only World Superbike race. I won the second race, so we were both ready for a few beers at the presentation ceremony that evening. The compere called us on stage to cut a special cake that had been made, and whenever he turned his back on us to face the audience I fired dollops of cake at his back with the cake knife. The audience were in stitches and James was almost wetting himself on the stage. The compere thought we were laughing at his jokes. 'I can't believe you are getting away with this,' James wheezed, but the guy was pretty pissed off when he discovered Victoria sponge all over the back of his brand-new suit.

It's fair to assume James was feeling a bit hungover for the golf the following day, which was stinking hot. It's also widespread knowledge that James only needs to step off a plane in a foreign country for his tummy to start rumbling. Add these two things together and it was a recipe for disaster. Sure enough, halfway around the course and miles from the clubhouse, his stomach started to churn. There wasn't even time to make it into the bushes, and you wouldn't want to be crouching down in the long grass over there unless you wanted a viper attached to your bollocks. So, there was nothing else for it but to drop his kecks and shit in the bunker on the 9th hole. Now what to do? His arse had exploded everywhere. So off came his shoes and he wiped himself down with his socks. This didn't quite do the job, so he finished off by borrowing the head cover off one of Brian's clubs. To give him credit, James wasn't going to leave this steaming pile of crap, socks and soiled Ping head cover for all to see. No, he was much too considerate to do that. Instead, he dug a hole in the sand and buried the lot. And then raked the sand, obviously. Can you imagine an unsuspecting local golf club member coming along a couple of days later after landing in the bunker? Then his bunker shot lands close to the pin, but so does this stinking bundle of shitty rags and he's wondering: 'Where the f**k did that come from?' You really don't want to know, mate.

I've had a laugh with Ian Poulter, the Ryder Cup hero, over the years. It started when I tried to wind him up when I discovered he had more than a million followers on Twitter. I was just starting out and had only 11,000.

'Oi, @IanJamesPoulter. How come you knock a little white ball around a field and have so many followers, when I've won seven world championships and only have 11k?' I tweeted.

Ian responded straightaway with some banter and then messaged me to ask if I had any memorabilia for his collection. It turned out he lived near Kev's daughter in Lake Nona, Florida, and Kev offered to deliver a replica helmet next time he was over. Poults was made up and put the helmet next to the putter that Seve Ballesteros used to win the British Open, plus signed pictures of Muhammad Ali and Nelson Mandela. In return, he sent a flag signed by all the European Ryder Cup winning team from the 'Miracle at Medinah' in 2012.

'What the f**k?' I told Kev when he brought it round. 'I send a signed helmet and he sends me a bloody flag?'

Kev was going mental, so I decided to wind Poults up and tweeted a picture of me holding the flag: 'Thanks @IanJamesPoulter for the flag. Should fetch a few quid on eBay.'

Kev received a message from Ian straightaway saying: 'Please tell me he is joking about the Ryder Cup flag.' The next time Kev dropped by Poulter's house in Florida – probably not by invitation, knowing Kev – he got payback on me by telling Kev to send me a picture of my helmet buried under a pile of old golf clubs he had thrown out. Sadly, I took the bait. We met up recently at the Goodwood Festival of Speed and the thing I like about Ian is that, just like me, his eyes give everything away – on the course and off. They looked like they would pop out of his head when he was playing in the Ryder Cup. And he did a lot of rolling of the eyes at our antics when he spent time with us at the ball at Goodwood.

Golf does not come close to being the sport that I dislike the most, though. That honour is definitely reserved for cricket. I'm the first to admit I don't particularly understand the game – and don't want to. I think I'm right that games can go on for five days and yet there might be no winner. How pathetic is that? It's no wonder only three men and their dogs turn up to watch most of these games. And these blokes obviously only use it as an excuse to get away from the missus.

'Just popping out to watch some cricket, luv.'

'Okay, how long will you be?'

'Five days.'

'Oh, okay . . . Enjoy!'

Apparently, they have invented a new faster version of the game called Twenty20. Presumably these matches only last for 20 minutes – which is still too long, in my opinion. I don't understand some of the terms either.

What's a run out? When there is no milk left in the dressing room to make a brew and someone has to run out and get some? Or is it that the batsman is so unfit that he's run out of breath? Silly mid-on – what's that? A semi-on that's funny?

My theory is that, because we invented it, the press and media feel obliged to cover it out of pity. Let's face it, no boy or girl grows up wanting to play cricket, do they? They want to play football, rugby or race bikes. But if they are not good enough at these sports, they have to try cricket. So we take pity on them and set them ridiculously easy targets. If you beat one country called Australia every 15–20 years or so then we will close down the streets of London, parade you around in an open-top bus, award you gongs, allow you to piss in the flowerbeds of Number 10, give you all your own TV shows, radio shows and newspaper columns, and then let you pedalo off into the sunset. That should make you feel better for the embarrassment of celebrating such a meaningless victory as though you have won the World Cup four times in succession.

I have met some great guys, don't get me wrong, like Ian Botham, Phil Tufnell, and Freddie Flintoff, and I have a laugh with a few cricketers like Michael Vaughan on Twitter, but they are always banging on about football instead of their own sport, not surprisingly. And it was a cricketer that I blame for my most embarrassing moment on TV.

I had been on *A Question of Sport* a few times already, but not many other TV shows, when I was asked to be on a special sporting edition of *The Weakest Link*, a popular general-knowledge quiz show in which contestants are voted off by their fellow contestants. It was hosted by the legendarily scary Anne Robinson. My general knowledge is not bad – especially on sport and music – but I still had to be persuaded to go on the show. I knew I would never live it down if I was voted off first, but I convinced myself that it would never happen.

I recognised a few of the other contestants in the Green Room, such as the boxer Audley Harrison, rower Matthew Pinsent and Paralympian Tanni Grey-Thompson. There was another big bloke standing quietly on his own next to the door and I thought he was on security, until I realised he was necking a few beers. He was eventually introduced as the cricketer, Andrew Flintoff. His wife Rachel immediately hit it off with Michaela while Freddie, as he is known, encouraged me to have a couple of beers for Dutch Courage. He can drink. I can't. And I was a bit merry by the time the show started.

The contestants all line up and Anne Robinson goes along the line asking questions. The group wins money for every question answered correctly, but you lose all that money when someone gets an answer wrong. The trick is to bank the team's money before someone messes up. I was towards the end of the line and most people answered correctly, so I banked our money when it came to my turn. So far, so good. My first question was: 'What type of bladed object is found in the office?' Scissors. This is a piece of piss. In the first round, everyone has two questions and I banked more money when it was my turn again. That always goes down well with the other contestants.

'What type of bean do you find in a Sambuca drink – a coffee bean or runner bean?'

'Runner bean . . .'

Shit – what just came out of my mouth?

'. . . no, coffee bean.'

'Wrong,' said Anne Robinson. 'It's a coffee bean.' Noooooooo ... I didn't mean to say that! Matthew Pinsent started pissing himself next to me. I wanted the floor to open and swallow me up. How the hell did I get that wrong? But it's amazing what can happen inside your head when you are in front of the cameras and under the studio lights. The pressure can get to you and questions that you would answer correctly 99 times out of a 100 at home can completely throw you. It's happened since on *A Question of Sport*, too – and on my home sport question. Sue Barker asked which American became a double World Superbike Champion in 2002. I thought she said 1992 and blurted out Doug Polen. 'No, it was actually Colin Edwards,' said Sue. I got some stick for that – from my team-mates on the show, my mates and the fans.

Then there was the time I was on the game show *Tipping Point* recently, with chef Marco Pierre White and *Coronation Street*'s Brooke Vincent. The questions are really not that hard, but I still managed to get a few wrong, including: 'What famous band is the tribute act Guns 2 Roses named after?' Ask me that in the comfort of my own armchair and I would obviously answer Guns N' Roses. But, oh no, not in front of a live audience and millions of viewers. I panicked and passed and the host, Ben Shepherd, just shook his head in dismay. Then Brooke passed a question over to me: 'The original mascot of which photo and video-sharing app was Ghostface Chillah?' I hadn't got a clue what the answer was, but I had to say something, so I said the first name that came into my head – I said Fred Flintstone, which obviously amused the live audience. The answer was Snapchat. Brooke wasn't much better, either. 'Which type of non-venomous snake is the title of a Nicki Minaj hit?' She answered panther! Me and Brooke were like two naughty schoolkids in front of the very serious headmaster, Marco, who really did seem a bit thick. I even beat him on a food question about the colour of broccoli. You would have thought he might have known that. I went on to win the show £20,000 for the NSPCC, which was a great feeling because I know how they can help many children's lives with that kind of money.

These mishaps were nothing compared to the annihilation I was facing after the runner bean answer on *The Weakest Link*, though. But all was not lost because Flintoff got his next question wrong. 'I've banked all the money here. I might have a chance,' I thought. When it was time to vote, Pinsent whispered: 'Sorry but I've got to put you down – that was too funny.'

'You'd better f**king not, mate,' I whispered back. My only hope was that people would vote for Freddie and I counted the votes in my head. 'It's a tie – four votes for him and four for me. That means it's up to the Strongest Link to decide. That was Tanni Grey-Thompson and she voted for Flintoff. Woohoo – I'm safe.'

'Carl, you are the Weakest Link. Goodbye,' said Anne Robinson.

'What? No I'm not, it's him. It's Flintoff!' I thought. I could have burst into tears. Not only had I got the question wrong, I had added up wrong, too. Those beers must have been stronger than I thought. The votes had gone 5–4 against me. It was like someone had kicked me in the guts. And they kept kicking me while I was down when the floor manager shouted 'Cut!' and we had to film Anne calling me the Weakest Link one more time. And then another time for good measure.

I skulked off the set and found Michaela and Rachel Flintoff rolling around the floor of the Green Room, pissing themselves. I was not amused. Nobody would accept that I knew the answer. 'Come on, we're going,' I told Michaela. 'I'm not waiting around for those public school Olympians that voted me off to take the piss.'

'Let's just see how Andrew gets on,' she said. Sure enough, he was next off by the time we were ready to go, but he wanted to go out on the town immediately.

'F**k that,' I told him. 'I'm going back to my hotel to hang myself.' In the cab back to the hotel, Michaela rang Kev and put him on loudspeaker, but they couldn't make any sense because they were both wheezing so much. I grabbed the phone off her, rang off and threatened to hurl it out of the cab window. Then I rang my manager, Neil, to tell him he was sacked for getting me on the show. He just pissed himself, too, and said he was going to give Mastermind a call straightaway.

The Weakest Link had been filmed in October 2002, but I had to wait three long, painful months before it was broadcast in January, quite late at night on BBC2. Not many people saw that show and I thought I got away with it. Then it was repeated primetime and, sure enough, the floodgates opened. I had to switch my phone off for a few days to wait for everyone to stop calling me a thick bastard. And it didn't end there. I went skiing a few weeks later in the Swiss resort of Verbier, where my mate Rob Sawyer owned the main hotel, called Farinet. After the first day on the slopes, we were in his hotel bar for some après ski and Rob got the first round in – a tray full of Sambuca shots, each with a runner bean in the bottom. Very funny . . . Twats.

I'm not the only one to regret ever having heard of Sambuca, though. As I lay semi-conscious in a Melbourne hospital bed after the massive crash at Phillip Island that ended my career in 2000, the rest of the lads were obviously so concerned that they went out on the piss to the popular Italian restaurant, Isola di Capri. It's not uncommon for the Sambuca to come out after the meal there. On this occasion, someone decided it would be a good idea to play Flaming Sambucas. You drink the Sambuca, light the bit left in the bottom of the glass, blow it out and quickly place it on your skin. The flames have burnt all the oxygen in the glass to create a small vacuum and the glass sticks there. All very well, in theory. And if your name is not James Whitham. And you haven't already had a couple of shandies. When it was James' turn, he left a bit too much Sambuca in the glass and left it burning a bit too long. So when he blew the flames out, the glass was red hot when he placed it over his nipple. It stuck there alright, but also seared a scar through his nipple which is there to this day. It probably didn't help that he has a fair pair of man boobs.

It's not the only time he has been burned, either. And it was former England rugby captain Lawrence Dallaglio doing the burning. It was at the opening weekend for a new restaurant in Verbier called La Vache. Rob, who used to own a hotel there, had called to ask me if I would like to chip in some money with a local guy and two other friends of his who I had met previously in Verbier – Lawrence and the singer James Blunt. Rob used to run some bars and clubs in London and Ibiza and knew Lawrence from that scene; and Rob's dad was in the army with James' dad. Apparently, Blunty used to ask Rob if he could play in his clubs before he was famous, but Rob wasn't too keen. The next thing you know he is selling out Wembley stadium.

Foggy, Dallaglio and Blunt – as unlikely a combination of business partners as you could ever hope to find. But it all came together and it's a pretty cool place, up on the mountain at the top of Les Attelas. (Mention my name and you'll get no special treatment whatsoever.) The three cubicles in the gents are themed around the three of us. If you are sitting on my bog, the walls and door are designed so that it looks like you are sitting on a bike on the starting grid. In Lawrence's crapper, it looks like you are in the middle of a scrum. And in James', all you can see is a microphone and a sea of faces from the stage, mainly young girls. James called me a cheeky bastard when I suggested it was taken at a Robbie Williams gig, not a James Blunt concert. There is also a pizza on the menu named after each of us. I wanted a spicy one, with spicy salami, red onions and chilli, but James got in there first, which pissed me off. So I was left with all the boring ingredients like Parma ham and rocket for the Foggy pizza. But at least it was Number 1 on the menu. The Blunt is at Number 9, which is probably the highest he has ever been in the charts in recent years. I'm not sure what's on Lawrence's, but I would take a guess at raw meat and offal.

I invited James over for the opening weekend, to do a bit of skiing and a lot of partying. Being a tight-as-arseholes Yorkshireman, he didn't want to pay for a hotel room, so I told him he could sleep at the foot of our bed on a camp bed. The first night was messy. Lawrence is one of the nicest blokes you could ever hope to meet, but he is also an animal and can drink more on one night than I can in a week. None of us could keep up and Michaela was first to sneak off to bed early. Me and James were not far behind and James was already buried under the duvet when Lawrence burst in, almost taking the door off its hinges. He tried to yank the duvet off Michaela, but she was hanging on for dear life. Then he spotted the body in the camp bed.

'Who do we have here then?' he said and lifted one end of the cover to reveal James' feet. Out came Lawrence's lighter, which he lit under his feet. After a few seconds, James leapt out of bed and was ready to smack whoever was responsible, until he realised that it was Lawrence. So, instead, in the most pitiful voice possible, he whined: 'Hey, stop it. That really hurt, you know.' James had no option but to go back to the bar and continue long into the night. I promised I would be down in a sec but managed to sneak under the Dallaglio radar.

The next day was the official opening and we were all as rough as badgers' arses. Me and Blunty didn't take our sunglasses off for any of the official photos, because we looked so knackered. He may have a posh-boy reputation but he can party with the best of them, let me tell you. Lots of media turned up and a few other celebrities like Heston Blumenthal. And then it all started again, like *Groundhog Day*. There was Premiership football on the telly in the bar back down in Verbier, but Lawrence hates football and was determined that nobody else would be able to watch the game in peace. First, he tried standing in front of the big screen – and he makes an effective obstacle. We all moved to the bottom of a long table, packed with empty beer glasses, for a better view and so Lawrence tried a new tactic. He ran at the table, jumped and belly-surfed down it, scattering glasses all over the bar. Sitting at the end of the table, with his back to all this and happily watching the game, was me. It was like a rhinoceros T-boning a meerkat. I didn't know what hit me until I looked up from a pile of broken glass to see Dallaglio's big, idiotic grin poking over the edge of the table. There's not much you can do to retaliate in that situation.

2

HAVE A HART SON

I am starting to see why Lawrence Dallaglio and other rugby players dislike football so much. One of my proudest sporting memories is England's Rugby World Cup win in 2003, when Jonny Wilkinson kicked that drop goal in injury time to beat Australia in their own backyard. It took a lot of balls to deal with that pressure and produce such a fairy-tale ending. I was in tears watching at home. Real men, real sport.

I'm usually crying for a different reason when I watch the England football team. Every major tournament, I tell myself not to get sucked in by the hype and thinking that we can actually win something. I don't mind if we get knocked out on penalties. There's not much you can do about that. So much seems to come down to luck. How did Portugal, for instance, win the last European Championships after scraping through their group in third place? How did Italy win the World Cup in 2006 after drawing 1–1 with USA in the group stage? The Italian side that won in 1982 weren't that good, either. How did the Denmark team, who were all lounging on a beach before Yugoslavia were disqualified, win the European Champion- ships in 1992? It baffles me. Yet luck didn't seem to play much of a part when Iceland, with a population of 53 people, beat us in the 2016 Euro- pean Championships. The 11 players who represented the other 42 Icelanders showed heart and soul – and pride. And pride really does seem to be the missing ingredient with England's very wealthy footballers.

I'm the proudest English sportsman who has ever lived and always had the English flag on my helmet and bike. Nowadays, English riders seem to try to gain more Scottish, Welsh and Irish fans by using the British flag instead. Really? Riders from those countries use their own flags. I have lots of fans in Scotland, Wales and Ireland – nobody ever said I should have been using the Union Jack. In fact, they respected me even more for being so proud to be English, just as they are proud of their own countries. I have even seen riders who live on the Isle of Man use the Manx flag. Come on, guys, really?

I was asked to appear in an advert that Carlsberg filmed before the 2010 World Cup at Millwall's ground, the New Den. It showed former England left-back Stuart Pearce giving a passionate team talk in the dressing room before the players walked through the tunnel lined with English sporting icons such as World Cup winner Jackie Charlton, the rower Sir Steve Redgrave, cricketer Sir Ian Botham dressed in medieval chainmail, footballer Sir Trevor Brooking, England rugby manager Sir Clive Woodward (there are a lot of Sirs in this list, aren't there . . . !?), boxer Nigel Benn, darts player Phil Taylor, athlete Dame Kelly Holmes, round- the-world yachtswoman Dame Ellen MacArthur (there are also a lot of

Dames in this list), and some random English entertainers like the band Kasabian and, most random of all, a half-naked Jeff Stelling. I was filmed in my leathers, getting on the bike to do a burn-out in the tunnel and fist-pumping the players before they took the field. The advert finished: 'It's time to join the immortals . . . If Carlsberg did team talks.' It was rousing stuff — an attempt to generate the type of passion our national team badly needs. But after a couple of days on TV, my bit was mysteriously cut from the advert, which pissed me off a bit. Apparently, some do-gooders had complained about motorcycle riding being linked to an alcoholic drink. Yep, that's right — you were obviously going to think: 'I've just seen Foggy on TV, I'm going to neck a six-pack of lager and jump on my bike.' Anyway, I made my mark because the burn-out left a big patch of rubber on the concourse and one of the Millwall stewards got me to sign it in silver pen on the way out. Millwall fans, look out for it at the next home match, if you are not too busy scoffing on your pies.

It's not so much the lack of pride that annoys me, and so many other people, about football. It's the lying, diving, whinging, cheating players who try to win free-kicks and penalties, or get an opponent booked or sent off — mainly by the teams from Europe in the Champions League. You can see why a rugby player, who never bats an eyelid about charging into another 18-stone wall of muscle at full speed and picks himself straight up to do it again, can't bear to watch these pussies sometimes. Google 'lying, diving, whinging, cheating footballers' and the compilations on YouTube will make your skin crawl. There is one clip of a coin, thrown from the crowd, glancing off a player's face. Obviously, that's unacceptable. But, after he goes down like a sack of spuds, the rest of his team all throw themselves to the ground, holding their faces. It's absolutely pathetic.

Do the governing bodies of the most popular sport in the world not realise that this kind of behaviour is turning so many people who once loved the game, like me, away for good? It's so hard for the referees, who are often influenced by the home supporters baying for blood if their star player has tripped over a particularly long blade of grass. So it's good to see FIFA starting to use video assistant referees, but there also should be a panel which judges players accused of cheating – and I'm available as a panel member. The punishment for anyone found guilty should be a public horsewhipping. That might make them think twice about doing it again.

Let's settle the debate about my football allegiance once and for all. You might think, as a shareholder, that my heart belongs to Accrington Stanley. I was given one share in the club when I was invited as a guest to a game a few years back, joining the likes of Sir Alex Ferguson, who also owns one share but had to pay £100 for his. It's now probably worth the price of a pint of milk at the time Ian Rush filmed the famous milk advert in the 1990s. I do look out for Stanley's results, but I obviously grew up supporting my local team, Blackburn Rovers, and often stood on the terraces at Ewood Park when we were in the old Third Division. Unfortunately, Rovers are now back in the third tier following a disastrous takeover by a family of Indian chicken farmers called Venky's, who own their country's equivalent of Kentucky Fried Chicken. I don't know all the ins and outs, but I do know they should get back to roasting roosters and sell the club back to anyone who has the interests of Blackburn Rovers at heart. So that's where my true allegiance lies, but most people from a small town also have a favourite big-name team and mine was always, and still is, Manchester United. George Best was just past his prime when I was young – an era when characters still existed in sport and it wasn't frowned upon to be photographed with a fag in one hand, a beer in the other and a good-looking bird on each arm.

Then Rovers caused me a problem when Jack Walker, a local steel magnate who used to do business with my dad's haulage firm, bought the club and appointed Kenny Dalglish as manager. Kenny took them back into the top flight. Suddenly, we were United's main rivals and people wanted to know where my loyalties lay. The truth is that I stuck with United – but for all the wrong reasons. This was the mid-1990s and I had started to dominate my sport. I won my first world title in 1994, when United and Rovers finished the season in first and second places. But I was pissed off with Blackburn, mainly because I felt that the town and particularly the local newspaper, the *Lancashire Evening Telegraph*, were not giving me the recognition I deserved. Manchester United invited me to games and I had lunch with their chairman, Martin Edwards, and manager Alex Ferguson. But it was a struggle sometimes to even get a ticket to a Blackburn game. I was self-centred and single-minded in those days (not the more mellow character I am today) and these little things wound me up and I shouldn't have let them. When Rovers won the 1994–95 title on the final day of the season at Anfield, as it turned out because United failed to win at West Ham, I should have been prouder of my hometown club. It was an incredible achievement for a small-town club and one that will never be repeated. (Leicester's title in 2014–15 doesn't count because Leicester is a city.) But Jack Walker must be turning in his grave at what has happened to his club since his death. The members of the Trust who sold the club to Venky's should be doing some soul-searching, too.

I still go to the occasional game, often with my mates. Remember Kev, the golfer-batterer? We first met on a trail-ride organised by CCM, a small British motorbike manufacturer owned by the Clews family, in the Lake District. It was the middle of the racing season and I didn't tell Ducati I was going, for obvious reasons. It was a stinking hot day, but I wanted to protect myself as much as possible. I was getting into my racing leathers when one of the other riders came up and said: 'What are you wearing them for? You don't wear leathers on a ride-out, you'll sweat your bollocks off. I'm Kevin Moore, by the way. I used to be a footballer.'

'Look, mate. I'm leading the World Superbike Championship right now and can't afford to get injured,' I told him. I was actually quite nervous around strangers at that time and probably came across as a bit stand-offish.

We reached the top of Coniston and I could see that this guy was pretty quick. I waited for a long straight stretch and went flying past him and gave him the finger, for good measure. But I didn't see the sharp right-hander. Over the edge I went, arse over tit down a steep slope and through a load of brambles. Kev was looking down, pissing himself. First rule of trail-riding: if someone comes off, you piss yourself first and ask if they are okay later. But I was as mad as a wasp and scrambled up the bank, then threw my helmet and gloves down. Kev obviously thought I was going to smack him one.

'Look, calm down, you idiot,' he said. 'You were telling me you didn't want to get injured, but that's what's going to happen if you carry on riding like that.'

'F**k off and just help me get this bike back up, will you,' I snapped.

Off we went again, and this time the race was on. Kev got in front again but didn't see a bog until it was too late. He tried to lift his front wheel up but it dug in, threw him over the top and he landed face first in the mud about 10 yards from his bike. It was my turn to piss myself and he took it well. From that day on, we were always going to be mates.

We stayed overnight in a log cabin and you always fancy a few beers after a good afternoon on the dirt bikes, so we headed off into the nearest town, Bowness-on-Windermere. This was at the time when I was getting recognised a lot and word got out that I was in town. Soon they were queuing round the bar for autographs and Kev was acting like my manager, keeping everyone in line. Next up was this young guy and his girlfriend, who was wearing a tight, low-cut T-shirt that didn't leave much to the imagination.

'Sign her tits, will ya, Foggy?' the boyfriend asked, proud as anything.

'I will, but the pen's not going to work – she's sweating too much,' I said.

Kev jumped in and, without asking, started rubbing her chest with his sleeve. The young couple were loving it.

'It still won't work,' I said. 'Her skin needs to be tight.' Up popped Kev to stretch her tits while I signed them.

'I could get used to this job,' he laughed.

It was a good night and Kev knocked on my cabin door the next morning, all bright and breezy, to tell me he was off. I wasn't used to drinking and wasn't feeling at my best, so I opened the door slightly and agreed that we'd go on another ride-out soon. He could obviously smell something funny and pushed the door open a bit further to discover I'd spewed in the bed and all over the floor.

As we now know, all too well, Kev used to be a professional footballer and played for Blackpool, Newport County and a Swansea City team which at one point was top of the First Division. He's always banging on about his manager, John Toshack, and famous team-mates like Tommy Smith and Ian Callaghan, who both used to play for Liverpool, and how he went on to play for Newport County during their run to the quarter-finals of the European Cup Winners' Cup.

Kev was a wind-up merchant back then, too, and was always causing trouble. When he was at Blackpool as a 19-year-old, their game against Sunderland was due to be on *Match of the Day* one Saturday night, which was a big deal in those days because there were only two games on every week. But Kev was dropped when the team sheet went up on the Friday night. He went straight out on the town to drown his sorrows and decided that, if he wasn't playing, nobody would. So he climbed up the scaffolding for the TV cameras and into the ground with his mate, another player called Brian Wilson who went on to marry one of the Nolan Sisters, carrying a rusty saw to hack the goalposts down. The saw was too blunt, so Kev swung from the crossbar and managed to snap it just as the floodlights came on. Two security guards with dogs were legging it across the pitch. Brian quickly whizzed the saw while Kev was flailing around, trying to free himself from the net. The dogs chased them back to the scaffolding and they were just able to scramble over the grandstand and scarper.

The next day, the referee almost called the game off and the BBC commentator, John Motson, was going berserk. But the groundsman managed to bring a set of posts from the training ground just in time for kick-off. News of these mystery vandals was all over the local paper and Kev and Brian were shitting themselves all the next week. Then, one morning after training, Kev spotted a bloke in a suit standing next to his car. Copper, he thought. 'Look, I'll take the rap,' he told Brian, and strolled over to the guy who, it turned out, was actually from Kev's insurance company because his policy was out of date. Never one to miss an opportunity, Kev persuaded the man to yank his arm round his back and throw him over the bonnet like he was being arrested. As he hit the hood, Kev pointed at Brian with his free arm and screamed: 'It was him – he made me do it.' When the insurance guy let him go, Kev pissed himself laughing but Brian was already in tears and didn't speak to him for three weeks.

I've never seen Kev happier than when he came with me to another *A Question of Sport* appearance and the Welsh footballer, John Hartson, sat down with us in the Green Room after the show.

'John, this is my mate Kevin. He used to be a footballer,' I said.

'Really? Who for?' Hartson asked.

'Blackpool, Swansea and Newport County,' Kev replied, loving the attention.

'No way,' Hartson said. 'I grew up in Swansea. I was always down the Vetchfield during the John Toshack era. Wait a minute, you're not Kevin Moore, are you?'

'Yep, that's me,' said Kev, just about creaming himself.

'I remember that goal you scored against . . .'

'Stop right there, John. I know exactly the one you are going to say,' said Kev. 'My goal against Watford in that 3–3 draw in 1978 when Elton John landed on the pitch in a helicopter before the game.'

'That's the one. Unbelievable. And didn't you play for Newport County with John Aldridge when they reached the quarter-finals of the Cup Winners' Cup? Am I right in thinking you had a trial with Liverpool, too?'

'Bloody hell,' said Kev. 'You do know a lot about my career.'

'I can't keep this up any longer, Foggy,' laughed Hartson. 'Sorry, mate, but I've never heard of you. Carl told me to wind you up when we were sat in make-up.' I was on the floor, crying. Then, to cap it all, Stuart Pearce wandered into the Green Room.

'Wait, a minute,' Pearce said. 'Aren't you Kevin Moore who used to play for Swansea?' The room erupted again. This was payback for all the times Kev had stitched me up – and so many others.

I always fancied myself as a bit of a footballer, a tricky left winger – a bit like Chris Waddle but without the mullet. My school didn't play rugby – Darwen Vale was not that posh – and I would have been too small, anyway. Your size often determines the sport you are good at and motorbike racers seem to be getting smaller and smaller, especially in MotoGP. Marc Marquez, Dani Pedrosa and Jorge Lorenzo are the size of dwarfs.

Oops. Am I allowed to say dwarf? Apparently not on national TV. I found that out during the filming of an episode of Celebrity Squares, hosted by Warwick Davis, who is, let's say, 'vertically challenged'. He asked me a question about my favourite bikes and I tried to be funny by saying that I assumed that his favourite bike was a mini-moto – perfect for midgets. 'Cut! Sorry, Carl, but you can't say midgets,' the floor manager shouted. 'Let's roll again, but you will have to rephrase that.' Warwick, who is a very funny guy, was pissing himself. 'Thanks, Foggy, you bastard,' he laughed.

I tried again: 'I bet your favourite bike is a mini-moto – even dwarfs can reach the foot-pegs.'

'Cut! No, Carl, you can't say dwarf either.' The rest of the celebrities, like comedians Vic Reeves and Bob Mortimer, were in hysterics.

'Sorry, Warwick,' I said. 'I'm just a bit nervous. Help me out here.' It turns out there is no politically correct phrase other than 'small people'. I didn't know that. And isn't this another case of political correctness gone mad? The only bit they used in the broadcast was a story I told about once coming out of a store in Manchester when I was nearly run over by a little kid on a Segway. 'I was thinking he's too young to ride one of those on the streets,' I said on the show, 'until I realised it was actually Warwick, who was doing pantomime in Manchester.' Phew. I finally got away with it. Back in the Green Room after the show, Warwick's wife, Samantha, who is also a little person, was on the ground – or very near it – in stitches. Michaela was hiding her head in her hands in embarrassment.

Anyhow, I always think that taller riders do struggle, because they push the front so hard and will probably crash four or five times a season because of that. My former team-mate Ruben Xaus is 6 ft tall and might have won the title in 2003 if he hadn't lost the front too many times. Chaz Davies and Scott Redding probably fall into the same category. Another team-mate of mine, Terry Rymer, was 6 ft 2 in. and nicknamed Too Tall Tel. But Rossi is around 5 ft 11 in. and it doesn't seem to have done him any harm.

I'm 5 ft 8 in., so not as small as some, but I guess it's small enough to be a jockey. And I was actually asked by one of the betting companies to train as a jump jockey to ride in a one-off race at Cheltenham. If it had meant turning up and jumping in the saddle I would have given it a go, even though it's a long way down from those things. But they wanted me to train for about 10 weeks and spending that amount of time around horses did not appeal. The cyclist Victoria Pendleton took my place and rode a horse called Pacha du Polder to fifth place in the Foxhunters Chase, which is pretty impressive, I think.

I don't like horses and they don't like me. How can you trust an animal that, when you put it in a field full of lush green grass, eats the one thing it shouldn't and costs you £600 in vet fees? Michaela's horse, Cassie, was a pain in the arse and impossible to ride on the roads because it was scared stiff of cars. The only fun I had on it was taking it off-piste on a public footpath – until I came across some Walkers.

Now Walkers are a strange bunch of people who only stay alive by sucking the joy out of anything that looks like fun for other people. Sure enough, the first group of Walkers I galloped towards started moaning and whinging. 'You can't ride that thing round here,' they shouted. And the Walkers have not stopped whining for the last 20 years, but now it's mainly when I'm riding my mountain bike up to Darwen Tower. I can't do anything right when I'm approaching them from behind. If I ring the bell, they get pissed off. If I shout 'morning', they get pissed off. They will either tut loudly or, in extreme cases, shout: 'You just frightened me to death.' Which is ironic because the worst offenders are old people who look like they have been sucking lemons all their lives and are quite close to death anyway. When the same thing happens to me, when I'm out walking the dogs,

I smile to myself and think: 'Good for you for getting out on your bike.' And a minority of Walkers do have their hearts in the right place. But the majority never smile – instead they scowl like you have just run over their pet cat. And you can't answer old people back. I would like to shout: 'Is it too much to ask for you to move a couple of steps to the side for a cyclist who has every right to be on this gravel track? Get back to moaning about the guy next door whose lawnmower is too loud, you stupid old bitch.' But I don't shout that, because I'm a good citizen.

Even when I'm on the way back down and approaching them in full view from 100 yards away, I'll be going too fast for their liking. 'Sorry, madam. I was genuinely unaware there was a pre-determined speed limit on this shared public right of way. Could you kindly inform me of the regulation velocity at which I should travel?'

Tut, tut, tut . . .

One of the funniest things I have ever seen on an enduro ride involved Walkers – and one of my best mates, Mark Winstanley, who is sadly no longer with us. You will get to know Mark quite well in this book, but for now let's just say he was a fun-loving, full-throttle, lovable rogue. It was a melting hot day and a group of us were riding in the Lake District – and we were lost. We knew we had to get to a certain point on the mountain but had gone the wrong way and there was no way we could ride up there from where we were. The only option was to get off and man-handle the bikes up, one at a time. After what seemed like hours of this, we finally managed to get the last bike up and we all collapsed on the ground, knackered and with steam coming off us.

Four or five Walkers had also arrived at the same spot, at exactly the same time, and were sitting down to eat their lunch – stunned by these daft bikers and probably thinking it served us right for being on their territory. Mark dropped down next to a big old bloke with a beard that reached down to his boots and was filled with bits of Kendal Mint Cake from earlier in the morning.

'You lot are idiots,' the Walker said to Mark, just as he was opening his Tupperware lunchbox. Big mistake. Mark leant across and grabbed his chicken salad barm cake straight out of the box and stuffed it in his gob, bold as brass.

'Idiots, are we?' Mark spluttered through his mouthful of food. 'Always remember – first up, best dressed! You haven't got a bottle of pop in yer rucksack, have you, fella?'

The bearded bloke and his Walker friends were gobsmacked and quickly scuttled off to find a new picnic spot, grumbling and moaning under their breaths. Tut, tut, tut . . .

3

OLYMPIC TRIP 'N' JUMP

This is what I think happened, anyway. The organisers of the first modern Olympics in Athens in 1896 were on a site visit to check why construction was behind schedule and over budget. They weren't to know that's the way it would always be with major sporting events – or with building a chicken coop in my back garden, for that matter.

Sure enough, the inspection committee found the labourers mucking around during their tea break, competing for the title of the fastest man on the building site. A start and finish line was marked out, and someone was nominated official timer on the sundial. The first guy was a bit nervous, though. He stood at the start and swatted a few mozzies over his head, but his mates thought he was encouraging them to clap. He almost started a couple of times, but hesitated at the last second, before finally setting off like the clappers. About halfway down the track, he stumbled and almost fell but he somehow managed to hop from one leg to the other, then lunge forward before finally sprawling flat on his face in a pile of sand. His mates were choking on their taramasalata butties. Epic fail. But the guy dusted himself off and tried to laugh it off, before angrily challenging his mates to do better. This gave one of the inspection committee an idea.

'Let's make this an Olympic sport,' he suggested.

'What are the rules?' asked his assistant.

'Don't worry about all that,' said the boss. 'Just make them run fast, stumble, hop, pretend to fall and then hurl themselves into a sandpit. The crowd will love it.'

This man was obviously a genius because the trip 'n' jump – or triple jump as it became known – became the first ever sport in the modern Olympics and has stood the test of time. Highly-paid elite athletes are still awarded a gold medal every four years for basically stumbling into a sandpit.

And that's one of the things that annoys me about the Olympic Games. Should the bloke who sweeps the ice while his mate shoves a few rocks around in curling receive the same recognition as the athlete who can jump the highest or throw the furthest? Michaela will be asking for a gold medal every time she mops the kitchen floor at this rate. Or the woman who teaches her horse to dance around her garden – does she deserve the same medal as the fastest swimmer in the world? Greco-Roman wrestling – what's that all about? And why isn't there a mixed doubles event?

All Olympic medal winners become household names overnight. That annoys me, too. We never really hear about the winner of the world championship the following year. Even the World Athletics Champion-ships receive only a fraction of the coverage and hype of the Olympics. So why does winning a race in the Olympics receive so much more coverage than winning a world championship race? It's the same competitors, the same achievement – beating the best in the world on any given day. Bring the best sportsmen and athletes from the world's top sports together to compete for the ultimate prize every four years – that's fine. Nobody is ever going to complain about watching Usain Bolt run another race. But let's not go overboard.

Having said that, I must admit I got caught up in all the excitement for London 2012. It was amazing to see so much British success on home soil. The Paralympics athletes were amazing, too – to have that mental tough-ness to overcome their disabilities and to train so hard is something that most people, myself included, would probably not be able to do. But I just find it hard to understand a swimming race, and some other Paralympic sports, in which people with an obvious disability are competing against athletes who don't appear to have the same disadvantage. It's very difficult to grasp all the different categories of competition. Then there's the ques-tion of Paralympic athletes competing in able-bodied events with aids, such as the blades used by Oscar Pistorius. It's a no-win situation for the Para-lympic athlete. If they do badly then that's what's expected, but if they do well then everyone says they were at an advantage. Pistorius didn't win, so nobody created too much of a fuss. And he probably won't be needing his blades for sprinting anytime soon, unless he needs to get out of the show-ers in a hurry. I always found him shifty and what happened to that girl – and the pain he put her family through – was disgusting and unforgiveable.

Nowadays, almost every sport is included in the Olympics and I see that skateboarding and rounders – sorry, baseball – will be included at Japan 2020. Poker and pole-dancing are now recognised as official sports, and so they might even feature in future Olympics. I tried my hand at poker last year and won a tournament for novice celebrities organised by partypoker. I was up against the Adebayo Akinfenwa, a man mountain of a footballer known as the Beast, Jorgie Porter, the actress from *Hollyoaks*, and the former topless model, Melinda Messenger. It was a struggle to keep my eyes on my own pair of aces, but I somehow managed to bluff my way to the charity cash prize. Maybe there is hope for me to be an Olympian yet. I quite like the sound of seven-time world champion and Olympic gold medallist. Perhaps we might be husband and wife Olympic champions one day, if Michaela takes up pole-dancing. To the best of my knowledge she's never had a go, but I would certainly encourage her. I'm all for her trying out new healthy, energetic pursuits. We would just have to make sure the pole's concreted in well. Only for health and safety reasons, of course.

Even though new sports are being added to the Olympics all the time, the governing bodies will not even consider motorsports. Is their argument that racers could gain too much advantage from having the best machinery? That doesn't make sense. Rowers use the lightest materials for their boats. The latest running-shoe design can make the difference between winning and losing a sprint race where every hundredth of a second counts. Think about all the genetic expertise that goes into breeding the best horses for show jumping. Is the horse not doing most of the work, anyway? And we all know how much science has been involved in cycling over the years – and I'm not talking aerodynamic helmets.

Cycling is still a sport with a dodgy image, despite the efforts to clean it up. There is always some rumour about doping and I feel sorry for the likes of Sir Bradley Wiggins, whose achievements are amazing but will probably always be tainted by Lance Armstrong and the other cheats in the sport. Armstrong was a huge hero of mine, until we found out he was a cheating bastard. I do follow the Tour de France, although I sometimes struggle to understand the ins and outs of the peloton tactics. One thing I do know is that Wiggins' achievement of becoming the first ever British winner in 2012 and then winning an individual Olympic gold medal in the same year was unbelievable. Sure, there were the usual questions about his medications, but the French seemed to take him to their hearts, wearing stick-on sideburns. Jake Quickenden, my future son-in-law, was first reserve for the Channel 4 show *The Jump* when Wiggins took part and said that he was very competitive, although it never looked likely that Wiggins was going to win and he pulled out towards the end with injury. Jake was pissed off, because it was so late in the show that the production team did not allow him to take Bradley's place, and Jake reckoned he could have won. I like Wiggins – he has that Liam Gallagher swagger. Chris Froome remains Mr Unpopular with some cycling fans, especially in France, and was spat at by one spectator, then had a cup of piss thrown at him by another during the second of his four Tour de France wins. I remember tweeting a message of congratulations after his latest win, which was amazing, and had a few comments come straight back about the secretive methods of Team Sky. His latest 'adverse finding' from a drugs test has certainly done nothing to improve his reputation.

There was nobody more gutted than I was when Usain Bolt didn't go out with a bang with a gold medal in the 100m in his final world championship in London. This was the greatest sprinter, if not athlete, of all time. With a name like that you are always going to be the best, just like Barry Sheene was born to be fast, or Tiger Woods the best golfer. If Usain Bolt had been called Billy Sidebottom, he might not have been quite so fast. (No offence to any Billy Sidebottoms out there who might be decent sprinters.)

It made matters worse that he was beaten by Justin Gatlin, who has twice been banned for drug offences. In sport, for me, it's two strikes and you are out – banned for life. But sportsmen who test positive for banned substances for the first time have to be given a second chance. The only time you don't deserve a second chance in life is when you have killed somebody. I suppose that means I'm in favour of the death penalty. You used to be hanged for stealing an apple, which is perhaps a bit harsh. But if somebody killed a member of my family, there's no way I would want them to be kept alive, watching TV in their cell and being fed and watered. I would want them to suffer, too – an eye for an eye – preferably with a long, painful execution. That's if I hadn't got to them first. But then they would have to execute me.

I'm convinced that Noriyuki Haga, the Japanese World Superbike rider, had no idea that a supplement drink he took during the off-season contained ephedrine when he was eventually docked points and banned for one round in 2000 after his urine sample tested positive. Sure, it's a stimulant and banned substance, but how much benefit can a motorbike rider get from an artificial stimulant? It's not as though you are in danger of nodding off during a race. Why dock his points for just one of the races at Kyalami and not the other, though? Had it not been for that drugs test, he may well have beaten Colin Edwards to the title that year. Anthony Gobert, the youngest ever World Superbike race winner, twice tested positive for marijuana and was sacked by his teams. Perhaps that's not cheating, but you really don't want to be on the starting grid with someone who is away with the fairies.

Until the sport of cycling can clear its name once and for all, there is one immediate step that all cyclists can take to improve their image. STICK TO SINGLE FILE ON THE ROADS. I'm a keen cyclist, but I get really pissed off when they ride two or three abreast and hold up the traffic. If you want a chat, stop for a coffee. If you want to be mown down, ride next to your mate and have a natter. Start treating cars with more respect and caution. Can you imagine the outcry if motorbike riders started riding two abreast, chatting away through Bluetooth? We should be trying to encourage more use of cycles and motorcycles in the big cities, so that traffic can flow smoothly – but cyclists don't help themselves sometimes.

There is actually an even better way of improving traffic flow on Britain's roads – get rid of all traffic lights. What's their point? At a roundabout or crossroads, you give way to traffic on the right. Simple. What's the difference between a roundabout and a junction? Pull up to the junction, look right to see there is nothing coming, then look left and then go. Simple. All traffic lights achieve is to make you sit there for ages when nothing is coming. Just check the next time the lights are not working at a busy junction – traffic flows just fine and everyone continues with their day without a problem. Switch them back on and there's chaos. Traffic lights also create a massive carbon footprint on the planet, both from the lights themselves and engines running on idle. See? I'm saving the planet, too.

Have you ever seen an Italian waiting for a red light to turn green? No, they just ignore them. I'm not suggesting that for one minute, because that would be irresponsible and it's something I have never done. Honest. Let's just experiment for one day – switch them off all over the country and see what happens. The roads will work perfectly. Trust me, I'm right on this one.

Another reason to encourage people to ride bikes is that motorbikes don't create as much pollution as cars. So I'm not sure that London's plan to slap the same £12.50 car congestion charge on bikes built before 2007 is fair. What about incentives rather than penalties? Why not encourage people to ride a scooter to work? A free Foggy T-shirt for every scooter sold? I'm sure I can come to some arrangement with the Mayor of London.

Come to think of it, cycling is the one Olympic sport that does feature a motorised vehicle – in the keirin 'race'. WTF? The way I see it, some bloke is out delivering pizzas on the first motorbike ever built but gets fed up waiting at all the traffic lights, takes a short cut and ends up riding into the velodrome by mistake. There is a sprint event on the track with around eight riders, who all get stuck behind his motorbike and have to wait for him to find an exit and f**k off. But this guy has never been on television before and is loving the attention. Eventually, one of the cyclists loses their patience and decides to overtake, the others follow, and the race is back on. Now the delivery boy doesn't know what to do. If he carries on riding round, he will probably be arrested for invading the track. So, when everyone is distracted by the sprint finish, he sneaks off through the warm-up area and back to the local Domino's.

That's not the stupidest cycling event, though. That's got to be the 'sitting still' competition – sometimes known as the individual sprint. The aim of this race is to go slower than your opponent. If you can go so slow that you come to a complete stop, then that's a bonus. Tactically, it's better to do this at the top of the banking, so that someone from the crowd can bring you KFC while you are waiting for the race to start. This happens when the other guy mutters something under his breath like: 'I've just shagged your sister.' He can see how pissed off you are, so he shits himself and starts pedalling like mad. Even if you haven't finished your Bargain Bucket, you pelt after him to teach him a lesson. Finally, the race is on – and is then over after one lap.

I'm a keen cyclist and I do enjoy watching it now and again. My point is that there is so much technology, engineering and science involved in training and competition, so why couldn't motorcycle racing become an Olympic sport? You could have the top three or four riders from each country using the same engines, like they are doing with Triumph in Moto2 in 2019. If that was impossible to pull off with all the different contractual obligations, it wouldn't be a bad thing for riders to stick with their existing manufacturers. It's not always the fastest bike that wins the race. You need the right combination of rider, team and bike. And on the day, especially in unpredictable weather, anything could happen. Maybe it's the safety aspect that puts people off, but motorsport is so much safer now. Please, though, let's not get silly and consider Formula One – or the Procession as I prefer to call it – for the Olympics. Carp fishing would be more exciting.

I guess everyone who earns the right to compete at the highest level deserves to have a crack at his or her moment of glory. And the Olympic Games is the biggest stage of all, although you don't have to win to write your name in the history books. Remember the Swiss marathon runner who staggered into the stadium in Los Angeles in 1984 and, five minutes later, collapsed over the finishing line? (No, I can't remember her name, either – and someone should check CCTV footage because it looked to me like she'd been down the pub on the Prosecco.) What about Eric the Eel at Sydney 2000? Or Eddie the Eagle in the Calgary Winter Olympics in 1988? All became overnight sensations for being shit – and good luck to them.

The Olympics can also kick-start legendary careers. I'm thinking Usain, Michael Johnson, Daley Thompson, Kelly Holmes, Michael Phelps, Chris Hoy, Seb Coe, Carl Lewis, etc. But the one that stands head and shoulders – bloody big shoulders at that – above all Olympians in my mind is Sir Steve Redgrave (even though all he had to do was row a bloody boat with a few of his mates). To win five gold medals (and let's not forget the one bronze) at five consecutive Olympic Games is a phenomenal achievement. It doesn't matter that they weren't individual golds – you still need the same level of commitment, technique, dedication, motivation and athleticism, but also that extra skill of being able to work in a team. And Redgrave's career proves my point perfectly. Nobody talks about his nine world championship golds. The true greats are those sportsmen or women who go out there and dominate their sport year after year – not just once every four years, and not just Olympic sports.

FOGGY PHENOMENA
10 true sporting legends
(in no particular order)

Usain Bolt

The second coolest man on the planet.

Sir Steve Redgrave

He rowed a boat.

Michael Schumacher

A bit special on four wheels.

Phil Taylor

Great wrist action.

Stefan Everts

Motocross world champ who made it all look smooth and effortless.

Dougie Lampkin

Awesome on a bike with no seat.

Michael Phelps

Went well in the wet.

Roger Federer

Pure Swiss timing.

Serena Williams

Reckon I could beat her, though.

Muhammad Ali

Stings like a butterfly, floats like a bee. Or something like that . . .

4

LEG-DANGLING SHIT

You may have noticed there are no fishermen in my Foggy Phenomena Sporting Legends. I realise there is quite a bit of skill to it, but you can only become a good angler by first not being able to fit into society. If you've never had a girlfriend, the next best thing is to sit next to a pond all day or all night on your own, pulling out carp and putting them back. My mate, the footballer Jimmy Bullard, is a keen fisherman. I rest my case.

When I had a go at the TV show *The Big Fish Off*, I found the carp-fishing challenge really frustrating. It's that lack of patience thing again. The presenter, Ali Hamidi, pulled his face every time I cast my line more than four inches from the opposite bank. How the hell could he know exactly where the fish were? My opponent, the boxer Kell Brook, was casting left, right and centre but his fish were biting – so my competitive spirit kicked in. I'm not sure how the editors found enough footage to use on TV between the bits that had to be bleeped out.

I know it's popular, too. Didn't Bob Nudd, who was World Freshwater Angling Champion four times, receive a record number of votes for BBC Sports Personality of the Year? He didn't win the trophy because the BBC decided that a campaign to vote for him run by *Angling Times* was against the rules. I don't suppose any rules were broken when Princess Anne won it for . . . taking her horse out for a ride one day. Okay, let's face it, I'm still sore that I was snubbed by the BBC back in 1999, when I didn't even make it onto the shortlist of names for the public vote.

On the train down to the ceremony, I read in the newspapers that I was being tipped for the award. I was already hoping that I might be in the top two or three, but I started to believe that I had a chance of winning – and then started shitting myself about my acceptance speech. The numbers for the phone votes were announced quite early on in the show. The names and numbers were read out one by one and I thought: 'Typical, they are leaving me to last.' Then the final name was announced and I was not on the list. Some big stars sat near me, like Sebastian Coe, Roy Keane and Damon Hill, looked at me and shrugged, as if to say: 'What's gone wrong there, Foggy?' The footballer Dion Dublin, sitting behind me, leant over and whispered: 'Where's your number, mate?' I could see Michaela in the audience and she gestured to me as if to say: 'I can't believe this.' I almost stood up and walked out, and probably would have done just that if I hadn't been wired up for an interview with John Inverdale.

'Congratulations on winning your fourth World Superbike title,' he said.

'Thanks,' I grunted.

'If you win one more, you might be in the running because World Superbikes is on the BBC next year,' he said.

I think I managed a disgruntled laugh and shrug of the shoulders before he moved on. I was convinced that, with my massive following including the 120,000 crowd for Brands Hatch that year, which I think is still the biggest single-day attendance at a British sporting event, I would have had a good chance of winning, especially as the eventual winner Lennox Lewis was viewed as being partly Canadian. We will never know. And I will never forgive them.

The voting system is different nowadays, because the phone numbers are announced in advance. So I knew that Jonathan Rea would do well after his third successive World Superbike title. Motorcycling fans are a loyal bunch and, when you added in his support from Northern Ireland, it was no surprise to see him come second behind Mo Farah. It will be interesting to see if he will go one better and if he goes on to equal or surpass my four World Superbike titles. I genuinely hope he does it. I have said many times that he's the best British rider of his generation and he's a genuinely nice lad, with a lovely family, too. Not everyone will agree with me that Jonathan is the best of the current British crop. The one box that he ticks that Cal Crutchlow perhaps doesn't is consistency. And I would have loved to see how Jonathan would have done with a regular MotoGP ride. I think people expect me to be pissed off that Jonathan is challenging my record number of titles, but records are there for breaking. I'm actually a bit embarrassed about my record. It should have been 70–80 wins and seven or eight World Superbike titles.

Back with fishing and, for me, there are only two kinds – river fishing for salmon and sea fishing. Fishing for salmon is tough, although I did manage to land my first on a stretch of river near Pitlochry in Scotland using a rod borrowed from Ian Botham. The salmon might be jumping all around you but will only bite at something out of anger, so you have to keep dragging the lure through the water, until they snap at it and are hooked. Fishing over the wrecks at sea is a bit easier. Just dangle your line over the side and when the weight and bait hit the wreck, you reel it back up part way and then drop it back down until you have a bite from fish like cod, pollock, conger eels, or whatever else might be down there. I like to catch something I can eat – and you never see carp and chips on any menu.

Sea fishing with the lads was becoming quite a regular day out, so Mark Winstanley bought a second-hand boat off the back of a lorry. I use the term boat loosely – it was more like a barge. The first time we used it, we launched off Knott End, near Lytham, to fish for sea bass. Within a couple of hours, the engine blew. I'm the first to admit I'm not the best seaman, so when it was still not fixed an hour or so later I started to get a bit panicky.

'For f**k's sake, Mark. The tide's turned – we're drifting out to sea,' I said.

'Now then, lad, do not worry yourself,' said Mark, as cool as a cucumber as he lifted a tarpaulin to reveal a small backup outboard motor. Within five minutes, Mark had it rigged up, attached a fuel can and we were on our way, cracking open a few more beers and admiring the coastline, except for Heysham Power Station. Half an hour later and we were still cracking open a few beers and admiring the coastline. But Heysham Power Station was in exactly the same place.

'Mark, either there are two power stations round here or we haven't moved an inch. We're drifting out into the shipping channel,' I shouted.

The motor was basically an egg whisk and nowhere near big enough to power a boat that size against the tide, plus we were nearly out of fuel. Luckily, Mark had a Mayday radio; or it would have been lucky if he'd bothered to wire it up. By this time, I was really panicking. We had a curry booked at our favourite Indian, but at this rate I was never going to taste Indian food again because massive tankers were bearing down on us. And Mark, who was battling cancer, didn't give a shit.

'I'm dying anyway,' he laughed. 'The rest of you can fight for the one life jacket.'

Thankfully, there was enough mobile reception for one of us to call the coastguard to come and tow us into shore. Even their boat struggled to pull us. The whole thing would have been embarrassing enough – until a picture of the rescue appeared on the homepage of the RNLI website. And guess who was right at the front of our boat, looking grumpy as f**k? Yep, me.

On another occasion, we were late back to the beach with the same boat and the tide was going out, so the sand was too wet to use a van or truck to pull the boat ashore on the trailer. Quite a few other people were in the same position and a tractor was going up and down the beach towing them out of the water. But Mark just reversed his truck to the edge of the beach and sat on the back, without a care in the world. I yelled at him to grab the tractor next, or we were going to miss our chance.

No need for the tractor, lad,' he said, as he hopped off the truck, unhooked a cable from underneath and started to unwind it with a remote control. Then he wandered down to the boat, whistling as he went, and attached the cable to the trailer.

'Up here for thinking, boys,' he smiled, pointing at his head while he winched the trailer and boat up the beach, 'down there for dancing!' We had to admit it was quite impressive – for about 30 seconds until the winch started to smoke and then cut out. We were all rolling around in the sand, laughing, and Mark's face was a picture.

'Get up, you stupid f**kers,' he yelled. 'If we don't get that tractor right now, we'll be going home without my boat.'

We held an annual competition in memory of Mark for a few years – the Mark Winstanley Trophy – held off Anglesey to celebrate his life. The rules were simple: the biggest fish of the day won the trophy. There were 10 minutes remaining of the first competition when Michaela hauled in a 30 lb tope, a member of the shark family. Five minutes later, I caught one 6 lb bigger to win the prize. It was actually quite an emotional moment and I felt Mark was up there, wanting his mate to win.

It's probably quite clear by now that I like to be around big characters. It's just a shame that these characters are disappearing from top-class sport. The more sport is on television, the more sponsorship it attracts. The more sponsorship that's available, the more the sportsmen and sportswomen are paid. And the more they're paid, the more they're scared of opening their mouths.

This is most true in Formula One. Gone are the days when James Hunt could win a Grand Prix and be on the piss before reaching the rostrum. The drivers are now like robots. They have to thank the team, thank their sponsors, thank the Lord . . . It's even difficult to tell who the best drivers are, because so much is down to the car and the technology – more so than any other sport. I'm pretty sure the best driver is Lewis Hamilton, but there are only two teams capable of winning a race, so it's hard to tell. Having said that, to earn a drive in the best car, or a ride on the best bike, you have to be the best. Lewis has also proved himself in all conditions, when the technology advantage is not so crucial. And you have to respect anyone who is willing to strap himself into one of those things and race at over 200 mph. So I do always look out for his results, but I could never sit down and watch a full race, and I just can't get my head around the fact that F1 is so much bigger than bike racing, which is so much more exciting.

Sure, technology plays a much bigger part than it used to in motor-cycle racing, too. In the good old days, you could just rock up at an event, load the bike out of a transit van and go and win a GP. If there was a problem with the bike or the tyres, you rode round it. It seems that the electronics take over now. My right hand controlled the throttle, not a mapping system.

There are things that can be done to minimise the advantages, like everyone running the same electronics in British Superbikes. It's got to the point, though, that even I don't really understand it all any more. And if I don't, then what hope is there for Joe Public? Of course, we all want to see improved safety. But you race *because* of the dangers, not *in spite* of them. You either accept that or go carp fishing. And once something has been invented that makes the sport safer, it can't just be uninvented or ignored.

It amazes me then, with this increased emphasis on safety and with so much more money at stake, that riders are still allowed to train however they want. Only last season, when Valentino Rossi was challenging for an incredible eighth world championship in the premier class, he broke his leg riding an enduro bike between races. Rossi is such a big star that even if Yamaha had wanted to write a safe-training clause into his contract, he could easily have refused. When I ran a team, I didn't stop our riders from training on dirt bikes, even though an accident at a local motocross circuit at Preston Docks could easily have cost me my fourth World Superbike title in 1999. Just three days before I flew out to Assen, I landed a jump all wrong, flew over the top of the bars and landed on my wrist. My immediate reaction was that my wrist was broken – and that my world title hopes were out the window. Luckily, it was just sprained and I was able to win both races at Assen, which pretty much clinched the championship. Looking back, it was a reckless and stupid thing to do, but at that age you feel indestructible. Now I realise that I'm out of my depth on that kind of motocross track, so I don't do it any more.

The best way to stay fit is to cycle or go down the gym. But if you have to ride motorbikes to stay fit, then the best way is to take out all the silly jumps and the bumps that put so much stress on the joints. Ironically, that's the type of track at Rossi's ranch in Tavullia – about 1.8 km of hard-packed dirt with changes of elevation and tight twisty turns. I've never been to Tavullia, but apparently it's a village that's just built around Rossi, with a big merchandise shop, a Da Rossi pizza place and a fan club next to the church. A couple of miles away is the headquarters of Rossi 46, the company that runs all his business activities. The 200-acre ranch itself has a farm, gym, vineyard and olive trees. That's where he does all his training, racing against the young riders in his VR46 Academy.

It got me thinking that we could do something similar in my village,

Mellor. Perhaps not the olive trees, though . . . The dirt-track at Tavullia is often referred to as a TT track, and I think we will see them grow in popularity. I want to build one in my fields for mucking around on a 125cc bike with the equivalent of cut slicks. You would be very unlucky to hurt yourself on something like that.

A few of the British lads, such as the Lowes brothers, Alex and Sam, are into flat-tracking and clearly push themselves to the limit. It's probably because Marc Marquez is a fan of flat-tracking. Are they doing it for enjoyment? No doubt. Do they think it will keep them fit? Possibly. Will it make them better road racers? Maybe, but not in my opinion. The fastest way around a race track is to keep both wheels turning using lean angle to maintain speed in the corners; not sliding all over the place and scrubbing off speed. None of this leg-dangling shit. It's not rocket science. Just watch Jorge Lorenzo. He was the best of the current bunch at carrying corner speed through lean angle, before his move to Ducati.

Yet there are always exceptions to the rule and Marquez rips up the rule book and chucks it out of the window. I love watching him, but he rides right on the edge and I wouldn't be surprised if he crashed in the first three races of next season. He is that unpredictable.

Perhaps all the leg-dangling comes from this flat-track training, because both Rossi and Marquez do it a lot. Someone once told me that I started it all off in 1993 in the British GP at Silverstone. Despite having never ridden the Cagiva before, I was second fastest at the end of the first day, without ever being confident of the gearing or tyre choice. Then I crashed on the Saturday morning and had to use the second bike for the rest of the day, which meant more valuable set-up time lost. Even so, I qualified in fifth and was running second behind Wayne Rainey after Mick Doohan took out Alex Barros and Kevin Schwantz in the first-lap carnage. I was closing in on Rainey for a couple of laps, but then the problems with the rear tyre and front brake started. Luca Cadalora came past me into second, but I hung on to third place until the last lap, when the bike started to misfire. It was only later that I found out that I was actually running out of fuel. I braked so late going into the last corner, trying to hold off Niall Mackenzie, that my foot came off the peg – it wasn't deliberate leg-dangling. From there I was just trying to urge the bike over the line, but Mackenzie sneaked through for third place which was a real kick in the teeth. That's still one of the most disappointing moments of my career. On another weekend, especially after that first-lap carnage and without the limited track time on a strange bike with all the technical issues, I'm convinced I could have won that race.

Training on go-kart tracks is also becoming popular – a bit like super-moto with slick tyres but smaller bikes. And that's important, because if you land a jump wrong on a motocross track it will bite you, and bite you hard. Mind you, flat tracks can bite hard, too, if you are on a powerful bike. That's what happened to me in 2017 at DirtQuake.

How can I best describe DirtQuake? Mental? Barmy? It's marketed as 'an alternative motoring festival that encourages a diverse blend of bike fans, dirt racers, millennials, grease monkeys, celebrities, custom shop designers, speed freaks and weekend warriors to celebrate their shared love of motorbikes'. Which means that you are just as likely to be lined up against a guy in a Marge Simpson costume as you are to be lining up against Carl Fogarty. There are lots of different classes, all racing on a dirt oval in King's Lynn, but there are plans to take DirtQuake, and its sister event SnowQuake, all over the world. I first gave it a go in 2016 and really enjoyed it. Then the following year it was televised by North One, the same production company that does such a great job with the TT, for a one-off show on ITV4.

I was there in my role as a global ambassador for Triumph and all I had to do was ride their bikes round and round in circles. What could possibly go wrong? I was down for three classes: the Street Tracker class on the Saturday; and the Hooligan class plus the Best of British class on the Sunday. For the Street Tracker and Hooligan classes, Triumph had developed a modified Bonneville with a 1200cc Thruxton engine. The other lads were on whatever bikes they could find, mostly 600cc single cylinders that were perfect for that race and that track with a set of wet race tyres thrown on. My bike was twice the weight and twice the capacity. Not perfect for that race or that track. When I opened the throttle, the bike just spun. I knew I would have beaten them on a smaller bike, but I was struggling and it wasn't too much fun to ride. I had a gentle crash in the first heat and tried to get back on, but the starter was broken. So I had to come in the top five in the next heat in order to qualify for the final that afternoon, and I managed to stay in the top three and go on to finish fourth in the final.

'I'm looking a bit of a dick here,' I told the Triumph lads.

'Don't worry about it,' they said. 'It's just a bit of fun – we just want to showcase the Street Triple tomorrow.'

Just a bit of fun? Not as far as I was concerned. When I'm in a race situation, I want to win. When I'm in *any* competitive situation, I want to win. Christmas Day at the Foggy household can be a tense place when the board games come out. *Mr and Mrs* is a favourite, especially because me and Michaela have a system of winks and nods, which I admit might be seen as cheating to some. That system couldn't help us in the real *Mr and Mrs* TV show in 2015, because we had some really tough questions. 'Who looks best in leather?' was one question. I obviously said Michaela, but she thought they meant race leathers and said me. I suppose you can't win them all.

I did think I could win on the Sunday at DirtQuake, though, despite a lively night out in King's Lynn with the other Triumph rider, Gary Johnson. He won the TT in 2014 on a Daytona 675R, the last person to win a TT race for Triumph. But this was his first flat-track event and he was struggling, even on the modified bike I rode the previous year – a 900cc version of the Bonneville/Thruxton – which I came second on and was a lot easier to ride. I was back on that 1200cc bike again for the Hooligan class, the most popular class, and won one heat and was narrowly beaten into second in the other. So I was looking forward to the final, which Gary didn't qualify for after crashing in one of the heats.

For the Best of British class, Triumph asked me to ride the Speed Triple for the first time. This has the 765cc engine that will be used for Moto2 in 2019. And if this bike doesn't win every award for its class, I will be amazed. It's fantastic and I'm not just saying that as a Triumph ambassador. I loved riding it in the Best of British heats, which I won. But it's a four-stroke that thinks it's a two-stroke – so not built to ride on a speedway track with racing wets. And it gave me enough warnings, especially after one of the heat wins when I tried to show off down the straight and it almost fired me off.

I was on pole for the final. 'I'll piss this,' I thought. 'There's only Gary to beat and I beat him easily in both heats.'

The flag dropped and I whacked open the throttle and the bike went sideways, almost taking out the rider who was second on the grid. Still, I was into the first corner in second place and knew I could catch the leader easily. Coming out of the second bend I opened the gas again and then 'Wrrrrrrrrrrrrp . . .' The back squirmed underneath me and the bike smacked me down.

I immediately knew something was broken. My first thought was that I'd messed up the plates and pins in my shoulder from the crash that caused my retirement in 2000. And I couldn't breathe. There was a stunned silence around the track when the ambulance turned up and I managed to give a feeble thumbs-up to the hovering TV cameras. But I knew I was in trouble in more ways than one. 'She's going to f**king kill me,' was all that was going through my mind.

Michaela and I were due to move back into our house the very next day after spending a year in one of the properties we usually rent out in Lytham, while our house in Blackburn was being completely renovated. That rental property had hit the headlines a couple of years earlier when a drunken 17-year-old dickhead from nearby Blackpool, who had never driven a vehicle in his life, decided during a burglary that he also needed a car for the night. Amazingly, he made it the five miles from Blackpool to Lytham without killing someone. Then he decided to turn into our estate, clipped the kerb, and smashed through our fence into the front garden before ploughing into the brickwork next to the front door. Luckily, there were no tenants in the property at the time, because it could have been a lot worse. The lad managed to crawl out of the car and, not content with totalling one car and the best part of a front garden, tried to break into the next-door neighbour's car. The guy spotted him and called the police. The newspapers had a field day because I was named in court as the owner, even though I didn't live there. But they weren't allowed to name the 17-year-old, which hardly seemed fair. He was given a year in a youth detention centre, which was not long enough if you ask me.

Lying in the back of an ambulance on the way to King's Lynn Hospital, I would have settled for a year in prison, but I knew I had to face the music straightaway. I called Michaela's mobile but it went on to answerphone and I left a few messages. She rang me back a few minutes later, all cheerful. 'Hiya. How did it go?' She obviously hadn't listened to her messages.

'I've really hurt myself. I'm so sorry,' I wheezed, trying my best to make it sound like I was about to burst into tears. 'I'm going to be in hospital for a few days down here.'

'Yeah, very funny, dickhead. The removal men called to say they will be here at eight o'clock, by the way. How did it go, really?'

I think it's probably best if we don't repeat the exact words she used when she realised I wasn't joking. I was quite shocked such phrases even existed. I didn't need to be told, either, because I was so mad at myself. I knew that as soon as the flag dropped, I would see the red mist. And there was only one way that was going to end up, on a bike with a power delivery totally unsuitable for that track. The first X-rays were sent away to Australia because there was nobody available in the UK on a Sunday evening. I was told there were no broken ribs but my lung was punctured, which didn't really make any sense. So a drain had to be inserted through my ribcage into the lung. I just tried to ignore what was going on and let the morphine do its job. Then, the next morning, I was told I had eight broken ribs, then it went to ten, and then back down to three ribs with multiple fractures. Plus my shoulder blade was split in two. But the doctors couldn't believe how quickly I was healing and I was released after just four nights in hospital. They told me that professional rugby players would have been in bed for weeks with those injuries.

It was a frustrating time at home, because I couldn't help with any of the unpacking or the jobs that I would normally have done. Then, to add insult to injury, the ITV4 show was broadcast while I was in hospital. I felt stitched up. The whole show seemed to be about my crash – there was nothing about the heats I had won or anything about the bikes and why they were so difficult to ride on that kind of track. A few other people told me that the show did me no favours, too. It made me look like I had never been on a bike before. I spoke to North One a couple of months later and told them how I felt. So hopefully I will be given the chance to put the record straight one day.

If I'm allowed . . .

FOGGY PHENOMENA
10 true sporting characters

Alex Higgins

Once stayed at my grandma's house in Blackburn. Liked a drink, apparently. Alex, that is.

Maradona

You've got to *hand* it to him, he was good.

Roy Keane

Named our Jack Russell after him because he was a gnarly little thing, too.

John McEnroe

Check the archive footage. There always *was* chalk dust.

Conor McGregor

He's Irish, apparently.

Lawrence Dallaglio

Man or beast? You decide.

James Hunt

Made F1 look fun.

George Best

Never stayed at my grandma's house. Liked a drink, apparently.

Ian Botham

Great bloke, just not sure what sport he played.

Dennis Rodman

The answer to North Korea tensions, surely?

5

Characters might be disappearing from a lot of sports, but you could never say that about the Isle of Man TT. I'm often asked to choose my favourite TT rider of all time and there's never any doubt . . . George Shuttleworth.

You don't remember George? This was the character played by George Formby in the 1935 film, *No Limit*. It's the best biking film of all time, if not the best film of all time. It's still shown in the hotels and bars during TT week and it makes me laugh every time I see it. It's basically the story of George Shuttleworth, who dreams of becoming a TT rider. He borrows a fiver from his granddad to take his bike, the 'Shuttleworth Snap' which he built in his garage, across to the Isle of Man on the ferry, but everything then starts to go wrong. He eventually wins the race, and the girl that he meets on the ferry, but not before a few hilarious scrapes, including my favourite scene when he crashes through the pub at Ballacraine with people diving for cover everywhere.

Waterworks, on the Snaefell mountain road, which was one of the spots where George Shuttleworth crashed, is also on the long list of places my dad, also called George, came a cropper. He was on first-name terms with the air ambulance people on the island, but he didn't suffer any significant injuries. Dad once crashed at the bottom of Bray Hill in 1982 but, instead of hitting a wall or a lamppost, just slid up the road. You would count yourself lucky to be able to tell the tale, let alone walk away with just a few cuts and bruises after going off at the bottom of Bray Hill. He was racing again, bandaged from head to toe, just a couple of days later.

His only fractures throughout his racing career were both to his skull, at Carnaby and Aintree, two of the safest circuits in the world. The second crash happened right in front of me and I was next to his bed when he came to in hospital, a few weeks before Bonfire Night. I asked him if it would be okay to go ahead with the bonfire if he was still in hospital. 'Aye, lad,' he groaned, 'but it might be an idea to have it in the living room.' The living room? Really? This was too good to be true for a 12-year-old Foggy, and I'm surprised I didn't take him up on it.

For the record, Dad was a decent racer. But he had a business to run and a young family to support and didn't take it too seriously until it was a bit late. Even so, Dad was second on Barry Sheene's old 750cc Suzuki – Barry's Flyer – in Joey Dunlop's first ever TT win in 1977, the 1000cc Jubilee Classic. This was the first year the TT was not part of the Grand Prix calendar. I was praying for Joey to break down and there was a glimmer of hope when he pulled in at Ramsey to check something on his bike, but he got back on to win by more than 50 seconds. Dad was also in second place behind Phil Read in the Senior race that same year before the bike seized when a stone went through the radiator. He seemed to have bad luck at every turn, and often it wasn't even his fault. For instance, his mechanics once forgot to tighten the back wheel and the chain came off. He set off first that year but didn't make it to the first commentary point. Another time, he set off with Mike Hailwood with a trail of smoke coming out of his bike because his engine was running rich. But he was flying, even though the brakes didn't feel right, which he put down to a new set of pads bedding in. Dad was catching Mike until his engine seized after three or four miles on the run to Ballacraine. The marshal there said: 'Have you seen this, George? The brake pads are glowing red hot.' His mechanics had put the pads in the wrong way round, so there was metal against metal. He was so lucky his engine seized, because he may not have had any brakes at one of the fast sections. Again, you don't often live to tell the tale when something like that happens on the Isle of Man.

It's not like I've never cocked up, though. When I was involved with CCM ride-outs, one guy paid for his son to ride with me for his 21st birthday present. The dad and Kev came along and we had a great day in the Lake District, until the lad had a puncture late in the afternoon just before it started pissing down. Me and Kev were like the Ant Hill Mob from Wacky Races but, after a lot of swearing and cursing, we fixed the wheel and set off back to Coniston in the dark. After a minute or two, the lad was pipping his horn and waving for us to stop. By now, I was cold and fed up.

'My front wheel's all over the place,' he said. 'Can you check it's on right?' It was fine, so we set off again. Two minutes later and he was pipping at us and waving again.

'For f**k's sake, there's nothing wrong with it, you big girl. Just get on with it,' I snapped.

The lad looked a bit upset but soldiered on, wobbling all over the road until we dropped the bikes off with the CCM mechanic, Dave, and said our goodbyes. The following morning Dave asked if we had a puncture on one of the bikes.

'Yeah, but don't worry,' I said. 'I fixed it while Kev was boring them shit-less with his football stories.'

'Did you lose any tools?' asked Dave.

'Nope, they're all in the rucksack,' I replied.

'That's funny,' Dave laughed. 'Because I found this tyre lever between the inner tube and the tyre.' Oops.

The most nervous I have ever been at a race wasn't when I was on a starting grid but when me and James Whitham were being filmed as the mechanics for Paul Shoesmith at the TT in 2011 for the *Hell for Leather III* DVD. I was in charge of refuelling and I knew from personal experience what could go wrong during a pit-stop. It was at the Spa 24 hours round of the World Endurance Championship in Belgium in 1992. My team – me, Terry Rymer and a French rider called Jehan d'Orgeix – were leading but being pushed hard by the Suzuki team, who were slower on track but quicker in the pits. I was due to take over from d'Orgeix and jumped on the bike just as the mechanic pulled the nozzle out of the fuel tank, squirt-ing petrol into my eyes. 'I can't see a f**king thing,' I yelled, 'Jehan will have to go back out.' By the time he was ready to set off 30 seconds later, my vision was returning so I dragged him back off the bike because he was the slowest of the three of us.

We won the race but not before an even bigger scare – the closest I have come to death on a race track. I was coming out of one of the fastest corners when I saw an ambulance treating one of the Suzuki riders, who had crashed when his engine blew, spewing oil out over the track. My bike started to slide and I realised I'd hit the oil and was out of control. If I had gone down, I would have slid straight into the ambulance and there would only have been one outcome. Incredibly, I managed to stay on and missed the ambulance by a midge's dick. Back in the pits, nobody had any idea why I was as white as a ghost.

With all this in mind, I knew there was no margin for error when we were responsible for Paul Shoesmith. Shoey, a good mate of James' who had come late to TT racing in his forties, just loved the event and ran his own team for a number of years. I've never seen James so serious, either, plus he had to slot in his commentary duties for ITV. With the camera crew in our faces and both of us shitting ourselves, it was all a bit of a blur. I volunteered to do the fuel but assumed that one of his regular mechanics had filled the quick-filler for his first stop. A few minutes before the start, I checked that the quick-filler was in position and realised it was empty.

'Who's filling the quick-filler?' I shouted.

'You're joking,' yelled James. 'Quick, fuelling closes in five minutes and you can't get any after that.'

Panic stations! One of Shoey's mechanics gave me a lift over to the fuelling station and we just managed to fill it to the brim in time, despite sloshing it all over the place. When Shoey arrived for his first stop, it all went as planned. I rammed the quick-filler into the tank and told the mechanic to get the bike off the stand when it was nearly full. I had my rag at the ready in case any of it went near Shoey, because the filler can stick in the tank when you are trying to pull it out and the last thing I wanted to do was spray it in his face. It was a textbook pit-stop and Shoey went on to finish 15th, his best result in a Senior or Superbike race. He was so chuffed to walk away with a silver replica trophy, to add to the 40 or so bronze replicas he picked up over the years. Me and James were so relieved, with high fives all round.

Just throwing it out there, but what about a compulsory pit-stop in MotoGP? The fans love to see them and it always livens up a race when the riders have to come in to change tyres in iffy conditions. Not one for the purists, I know, but good teamwork is an important part of any success. Perhaps it could be something for Moto3 and Moto2, or some of the support classes for WSBK?

Back to the Isle of Man. Dad always said he couldn't beat Joey Dunlop there, but could beat him at other road circuits like the Ulster GP and the North West 200, where Dad's best result was second when just pipped over the line by Charlie Williams. He did beat Joey once in the Southern 100 on the Isle of Man in 1979, when Joey ran on through an open gate and into a field. It could have been a lot worse if the gate had been closed, as it usually was. Instead, it was like a scene from *No Limit*, with my dad on the road looking over the stone wall at Joey trying to stay upright in the middle of a field. 'The bugger's not going to go down,' my dad thought. Joey did fall, unhurt, but wasn't able to use his main bike for the big race later in the week, which Dad went on to win.

He was also really unlucky not to win the Senior race in 1981, when it was run over two days because of bad weather. Dad was running fourth, and close to the leaders, but the race was stopped after two laps because of the worsening conditions. Some people thought the restart, the following day, should have been run over four laps with the previous day's two laps still counting. But it was decided to run the full six-lap race from scratch. The weather was crap again, but Dad was second behind Mick Grant when he crashed at Braddan Bridge on the fifth lap. Somebody worked out that if the restart had been run over four laps, then Dad would have won on aggregate. He's a bit bitter to this day that Granty tried so hard to stop the original race when he was struggling. Tragically, the Aussie rider Kenny Blake was killed in a crash on that fifth lap, too.

Dad was also going really well in the British Grand Prix in 1977 and flew past the legendary Giacomo Agostini before crashing at the end of the first lap, when a top-six finish was definitely possible. But probably his biggest claim to fame was being Mike Hailwood's team-mate for one of the greatest comebacks in sporting history.

Hailwood was a hero to my dad. His first TT win came in the Lightweight class in 1961 and he went on to win 12 TTs, including the epic 1967 Senior win against his big rival, Agostini, in which he set a lap record which stood for eight years. 'Mike the Bike' won nine Grand Prix titles, five in 500ccs, before Honda pulled out of Grand Prix racing in 1968, paying him £50,000 – a huge amount of money in those days – not to ride for any other manufacturer.

He'd already had one spell driving Formula One cars, between 1963 and 1965, while he was still racing bikes and, after a few years of accepting occasional rides at races like Daytona 500, he returned to Formula One in 1971 and was probably most famous for trying to pull Clay

Regazzoni out of his burning car in the 1973 South African GP. Mike's driving suit caught fire and a marshal put it out with an extinguisher before he went back to rescue Regazzoni, showing incredible bravery for which he was awarded the George Medal.

So, when Hailwood shocked the motorsport world by announcing, at the age of 38, he was returning to the TT in 1978 to ride a Ducati 990S after 11 years in the bike-racing wilderness, it was a big deal for Dad to be in the same team as arguably one of the greatest riders of all time. Nobody gave Mike a cat in hell's chance of being competitive, but he won the Formula One race and set a new lap record. He won again the following year in the Senior race, when he switched to a Suzuki and Dad jumped on Hailwood's Ducati – which he promptly crashed at Signpost Corner. Amazingly, after all those bangs to the head, Dad is still as fit as a fiddle and looks 55, not 75. Lots of people ask why he never goes back to the TT, or to bike shows, but he's a lot happier doing odd jobs for people in their gardens.

So I grew up with the TT in my blood. It was like a second home to me. I don't remember much about school, but I do remember every minute of that extra week off school each year to go and watch Dad during TT fortnight. And when I started racing I could not wait to get to the island for the first time. It wasn't for the TT, but for the Manx GP which was run on the same course but later in the year. I had gone out there a few days early to do around seven or eight laps every day in the car, so that I would know where I was going. In hindsight, it was a waste of time because by the time I'd hit the bottom of Bray Hill, I might as well have been there for the first time. It was so different on a bike compared to inside a car. I still wanted as much track time on the bike as possible for the 250cc newcomers' race, so went out in every session including one damp and misty session where nobody could tell where they were going. I passed the other guys in newcomers' orange jackets in the first few laps but, all of a sudden, one of them came flying back underneath me at Ballacraine and nearly took my front end.

'Who the f**k is that dickhead?' I thought. I caught up to him, drafted alongside him on Sulby Straight and looked across angrily. I saw a weird-looking thing with a bright-red face and one big eye in the middle of his forehead. 'What the f**k's going on there?' I thought, as I pulled past him. Race on! Over the mountain section, we could barely see 20 yards in front of our faces, and how we are both here today I will never know. We pulled into the pits – me first, obviously – and I went up to introduce myself.

'That was a laugh, you nutter,' I said. 'I'm Carl Fogarty, good to meet you.'

'Too right. I'm James Whitham. See ya later, I'm off out for another lap.'

I had heard of him but never seen him on a bike before. And I thought: 'I'll have to watch out for him in the race, because he can ride.' I needn't have worried. I won the race quite easily but didn't see James anywhere, even in the pits. I asked around what had happened to him and was told that he had crashed over the mountain when he went back out during that practice session – setting the tone for the rest of his career.

James was always my best mate in racing and is still one of my best friends. We did a chat show together for quite a few years called 'Foggy and Whit' and one of our best stories was about his appearance at the Goodwood Festival in 2005. It's now one of the biggest events in the UK motorsport calendar and all the big names turn out. These stars of past and present ride various iconic bikes and drive racing cars up the hill, per-forming a few tricks for the crowd.

James was in impressive company that year, including Mick Doohan, Kevin Schwantz, Giacomo Agostini and Luigi Taveri, who won three 125 GP championships in the 1960s. James was riding the ValMoto Triumph Daytona that New Zealander Bruce Anstey rode to victory in the 2003 Supersport TT. James was last to go in his group and, after waiting around for everyone else to finish, he was bored and tried to liven things up by pulling a stand-up wheelie, which he was very proud of, while waving to the crowd. But he forgot the tight bend back into the holding area at the top of the hill and, coming down out of the wheelie, crashed straight into the gate post. His helmet was pushed back into his nose and there was blood everywhere, and probably a couple of teeth floating around. A couple of the riders who knew what James was capable of, like Schwantz and Mick Grant, were first on the scene and were genuinely worried. But by the time James could focus, lying on his back in the paddock in a pool of blood, all he could see was this line-up of racing legends like Doohan and Agostini and Taveri staring down at him and thinking: 'Who the f**k is this idiot?'

That wasn't the worst bit of it for James. He knew he would have to repair the bike – you bend it, you mend it. But the only person who might have had the necessary parts was Jack Valentine, the ValMoto team owner, who had just become the manager of my race team. We were racing in Misano that weekend, so James knew that this would soon get back to me. I was back at the hotel when I got a call from Jack and thought: 'What's wrong with our bike now?' Ten minutes later, when I could finally breathe again, I was able to tell Michaela that James had only gone and crashed at the one event it was almost impossible to crash at.

As we all know, crashing at the Isle of Man is no laughing matter. Even before I started racing there, I had been exposed to tragedy when Tony Dickinson, the dad of my motocrossing mate, Gary, who was best man at our wedding and became a mechanic for my race team, was killed at the Southern 100. Just a few years later, in 1986, I was there as a racer, but fear didn't enter my head. You simply can't start thinking about crashing, or you would never get on the bike and race. You also need luck on your side, though, and I had a big slice of luck in my very first TT race. I was lying around sixth when my bike seized up on the far side of the island. As I was waiting for assistance, I heard some horrible screams from about a mile further back down the road. A helicopter had landed in a field to pick up an injured rider but spooked a horse in the next field. It jumped out onto the road and was hit by a rider called Gene McDonnell, who was just about to come past where I was stranded. Gene and the horse were killed in one of the worst accidents seen at the TT. My girlfriend at the time was standing next to Gene's girlfriend in the pits and saw her break down in hysterics. Yet I managed to put all this out of my head and go out for the next race.

The only time that tragedy ever really freaked me out was three years later when a lad who I'd enjoyed a few beers with earlier in the week, Phil Hogg, was killed in the final practice. I pulled out of the Supersport race and just wanted to go back home to Blackburn. Both my dad and Michaela tried to talk to me, but it wasn't until I received a message from Phil's dad, telling me that his son would have wanted me to race on, that I realised that my actions weren't going to change what had happened. I came fourth in that Formula One TT race and, on a bike I borrowed to learn the circuit, was also fourth in the Junior TT, won by Johnny Rea, the dad of World Superbike rider Jonathan Rea. I also had my first podium on another borrowed bike for the Ultra Lightweight race, won by Joey's brother, Robert Dunlop. But the guys to beat that week were Steve Hislop, a fast road-racing specialist from Scotland, and another fast lad called Dave Leach, a softly spoken but very brave rider.

This was the last year that riders set off in pairs, and me and Dave were together, numbers 7 and 8, 10 seconds behind Hizzy on the road for the 750cc production race. We caught him up by the final lap and I knew that if I could just hang on to them through the fastest sections, where the road racers had the advantage, I would come into my own over the mountain, which suited my short-circuit racing style better because you could see the bends coming up. When I overtook Hizzy, I waved back at him as if to say, 'Stay back, it's not your race now', hoping he understood what I meant. But Dave had other ideas and came back alongside me. I was able to hold him off with some short-circuit scraping through Signpost and Governor's before pulling 1.8 seconds. It was crazy riding, even if I say so myself. By beating Hizzy, who won three races that year and became the first rider to lap at over 120 mph, I had announced myself as a top rider on the road racing scene.

That RC30 was given to me by Honda for winning and I sold it to a wealthy local businessman called Dale Winfield, who ran a discount shoe business and owned a massive collection of bikes, including the RC30 I won my first world title on, the Formula One TT in 1988. The RC30 was an important bike in my career. It may actually have held my career back on the short circuits, because the front-end handling was so bad. At certain corners of certain circuits, it just rolled and rolled and I had to adapt my knee style just to keep the thing up. But it looked stunning, was the fastest thing out there and the engine was bulletproof. By 1991, it was probably past its sell-by date but, in some ways, it did me good to learn World Superbikes the hard way.

When Dale came to pick up that first RC30, he spotted an old bike covered in grass and nettles, wedged between the shed and the garage. This was my first ever motorbike, which had been custom-made by a local dealer called Ken Martin for his son, Chris. It had a Honda C50 engine, three speeds, no clutch and a straight-through pipe that pissed everyone off because it made the bike so noisy. I would pretend I was Agostini when I down-shifted on a makeshift track which I created at the back of the paddock at Aintree while Dad was racing. That engine would have started the career of many a rider and we often used to dig this monkey bike out and start her up. But when Dale came round, it was just a rusted heap of junk, with the swing-arm cracked in two. Nevertheless, he threw it on the back of the truck with the RC30 and I didn't think anything more of it until Dale passed away a couple of years ago and his wife rang me.

'Remember that little bike Dale picked up back in 1989?' she said. 'Just before he died, he told me to make sure I got it back to you.' What a lovely gesture, from a genuine and generous bloke.

I picked it up from his warehouse the week after his funeral and tweeted a picture of it, which *Motor Cycle News* picked up on. Then I received a call from James Hewing at the National Motorcycle Museum asking if they could restore it as a promotional project. When they presented it back to me at one of their open days, it looked and sounded just as it had nearly 40 years ago when I was about nine or ten. It now has pride of place in my garage.

I had expected that the trophy from that first TT win would take pride of place in the cabinet, too, but I was really disappointed when I only received a shitty little plastic thing and not one of the amazing, iconic silver statue trophies. It made me even more determined to get my hands on the big ones, the Formula One and the Senior. The following year was the first time I tried to get in another rider's head – and it worked on Hizzy, my team-mate at Honda. After his performance in 1989 he was the man to beat, but I was telling anyone who would listen that he didn't stand a chance. So I then had to go out and make it come true. Even before the Formula One race, he was complaining that I was riding dangerously and I knew he didn't like setting off before me on the road. By the second lap, I had closed the 20 seconds and Hizzy soon retired with a problem with his brakes. Interestingly, his mechanics later claimed to know nothing about any problem.

It was the biggest win of my career and I was still on a high five days later for the Senior race. The conditions were terrible, but I soon reeled Hizzy in and managed to pull a 22-second lead on the first lap, which was some going. All I then needed to do was to stay upright and, coming down towards Creg ny Baa on the final lap, I had tears in my eyes. After seeing my dad try to win this race so many times and knowing how much it meant to so many people, this was such an emotional moment and that double win remains one of the highlights of my career.

Yet that's not the TT race that everyone remembers. That came two years later and was voted the greatest race ever during the 100th-anniversary celebrations of the TT. No prizes for guessing who my main rival was again. Our team manager, Neil Tuxworth, had been forced to hold me back for a few seconds during a pit-stop the previous year, so that me and Hizzy were not on track together during the Formula One race. He was scared we were going to take each other out. I had electrical problems all the way round for my only race that year, as my priority had switched to World Superbikes and I was starting to think that the risks of the TT didn't match the rewards on offer. So I fully expected that 1991 race to be my last at the TT but, as a privateer in 1992, I needed the money to fund my World Superbike campaign. Yamaha were paying me £6,000 to ride the OW01 and I was also receiving another £6,000 appearance money from the Isle of Man Tourist Board. With potential prize money, it was a lot of cash in those days.

I was leading the Formula One race by around 35 seconds when my gearbox went at the Bungalow on the fifth lap and I had to coast down the mountain. Then the engine seized in the Supersport 400. So the pressure was on for the Senior race, and Hizzy was also feeling the pressure as he was without a win that week, too. I was number 4 and Steve was number 19, so he was more than two minutes behind me on the road. My first signal said P1 + 1. Who was that? Maybe Phillip McCallen? It wasn't until my first pit-stop that I realised it was Hizzy. He took the lead on lap three, but I took less time on my next pit-stop and pulled some time back. By now my bike had started to fall apart. One of the clocks was hanging out, the rev counter wasn't working, there was brake fluid everywhere, the screen was broken and my rear shock had softened off. Apart from that the bike was mint! But it was still nip and tuck for the next couple of laps before Hizzy's lead stretched to nine seconds on the last lap. I knew that was too much to pull back, especially with the straight-line speed of the

Norton. He was going through the speed at 185 mph to my 168mph. Then my exhaust blew. Anyone else would have pulled in. 'The quicker I go, the faster I can get off the bike,' I thought, which perhaps wasn't the smartest plan. I managed to make it back to the pits and, when one of my mechanics shook my bike back, the sprocket bolts, which had sheared off, fell out of the fairing. The countdown to Hizzy's appearance started: '10, 9, 8, 7 . . . Here he is now 6, 5, 4 . . . Hislop has won by four seconds.' Bastard. Still, I managed to set a new outright lap record of 123.61 mph on a bike that wouldn't have completed another lap – a record which stood for seven years. Not bad for my last ever lap round the TT.

Or was it the last? When I see riders set off down Glencrutchery Road, people often say to me: 'I bet you're glad you're not doing it any more.' They are so wrong. It means so much more to me now than it did when I retired from World Superbikes. The magic of the place came flooding back when I went there for the 100th-anniversary celebrations in 2007. Now the TT results are the first I look out for if there's a clash with WSBK or MotoGP. And I love all the traditions, like stopping off at Fairy Bridge and saying hello to the fairies for luck.

'Come back, I dare you,' the island whispers. It's like a spiritual calling – a draw, a magnet. And I'm half-tempted to do one of the Classic races . . . although I think the chances of Michaela ever speaking to me again would be very low.

FOGGY PHENOMENA
10 racers

Kenny Roberts

My all-time hero as a kid.

Mike Hailwood

The greatest comeback to win the TT in 1978.

Jarno Saarinen

Could have been one of the greats. Robbed of more world titles.

Wayne Rainey

The ultimate professional, a thinking man's rider.

Valentino Rossi

Dominated the modern era.

Giacomo Agostini

On the fastest bike, but that normally means you're the fastest rider.

Barry Sheene

Catapulted the sport outside of motorcycling.

Mick Doohan

The main man of my era. Would have won seven world titles, if not for injury.

Marc Marquez

Already up there with the greatest ever, in my opinion.

IT'S TT TIME II

The big names of the TT come and go, but this is one event that manages to maintain a grassroots feel even though the riders have now become stars in their own right again. This is down to the TV coverage, which is bringing the spectacle of the TT into the living rooms of people all around the world. No doubt they're all spluttering into their cuppas thinking: 'Woah! What's all that about?' The drones, on-board footage and amazing super-slow-motion shots take the fans as close to the action as possible without actually being there. But nothing will ever beat being there in person.

So in the summer of 2015, after an incredibly busy few months following a certain TV reality show, I told my manager to clear the diary for a week. I was taking my mates to the TT – and doing it properly. I wanted to rent a house for the week, but it was all about location, location, location. When I spotted what looked like the ideal place online, I flew over for the day to check that everything was perfect. The house was near Ramsey, with a big garden for barbecues and a stone wall, perfect for a scaffold grandstand to watch the action from. The bikes would come from the right, fire over a small jump and then approach a fast right-hander before shooting away to School House Corner. It was also not one of the most dangerous spots on the TT circuit. Fans watch short-circuit races at points of the circuit where there will be overtaking and crashes. Some may not like me saying that, but it's human nature. Of course, nobody wants to see bad injuries, but crashes are exciting. Not at the TT, though. You feel sick whenever you hear of a crash over the tannoy and there's a collective sigh of relief when it's reported that the rider is unhurt. At the TT, the thrill comes from the sheer speed of the bikes flying past within inches of your face. The safety of the fans is often in the hands of the riders – and that adds to the thrill.

The sun shone all week, the tinnies were in constant supply, the barbe-cue sizzled, the action was awesome – and I don't think Ramsey knew what had hit it. It was three mates in, three mates out, with me there constantly. And I don't have the stamina for that amount of drinking. By Thursday, when I was interviewed on the start line for ITV4, I looked and sounded like I felt. F**ked. And the biggest drinkers arrived on that day, including my next-door neighbour and mate, Chris Monk. If any TV com-pany wants to find a British equivalent of the Osbournes, then look no further than the Monks. I say next-door neighbours, but they actually live about three fields behind us, further up the hill. Chris often reminds me that he looks down on me on a daily basis. He runs a waste management company with his wife, Louise, who Michaela calls the Beast, due to her legendary capacity to drink alcohol without getting pissed. Wherever there's muck there's brass. Their son, Jack, is about 14 going on 40 and already owns a flock of around 100 purebred sheep. There is never a day goes by without some calamity up there. For instance, you wouldn't be surprised to turn up the drive and find them trying to stop their pig shagging a goat with its head stuck in a fence.

Just before the TT trip, the latest trauma to hit the Monk household was another visit to hospital for Chris, who had snagged his arm on a barbecue and opened up a nasty gash which needed quite a few stitches. Despite this, he was straight out on the beers that first night on the island, but I badly needed an early night and sneaked back to the house. When Chris eventually staggered out of Bar Logo in Ramsey at 11 pm, he asked a couple of friendly coppers for some help in remembering where he was staying.

'It's that place Carl Fogarty has rented,' he told them.

'Hop in, we know where you mean, we'll give you a lift,' they said.

He was dicking about all the way home, trying to grab their hats from the back seat. The coppers woke the whole house up when they dropped him off, because they wanted to make sure he was actually staying with us.

'You might want to get his arm checked out as soon as possible,' one of the coppers said. Chris had probably fallen into a wall because the stitches had burst and there was blood everywhere. The arm was still a mess in the morning and we only had a short window of time to take him to hospital in Ramsey before the roads were closed at 9.30am for the racing. But when we arrived, the hospital was shut. Unbelievable. The busiest week for accidents in the year. We could see a receptionist down the corridor and banged on the window to get her attention.

'Hiya, Foggy,' she said, opening the door. 'We're shut for the next few days for the racing.'

'I can see that,' I said, 'but we can't leave my mate's arm like this.'

'Well, I suppose one of the nurses could stitch it up again, but there's no doctors here to give him any anaesthetic. He'll just have to grin and bear it.'

Chris reluctantly agreed. He did bear it, but he didn't grin. He howled like a banshee when the nurse stuck the needle into the wound, although I think the alcohol from the night before helped a bit. While they were bandaging it up, another old bloke turned up at the door. He had travelled from the other side of the island to give blood. If a Manxman says he is going to the other side of the island, his friends ask how many weeks he is going for. It just doesn't happen, even though it's only a 30-minute trip. Nobody ventures that far from home. When he learned that Chris had only been treated because the nurses recognised me he stormed off, scuttling off back to his lonely home on the Calf of Man, grumbling: 'That's bloody ridiculous.' I loved that week and would love to do it again soon. Only I have a feeling that the lovely couple we rented the house from might not be too keen to have us back.

After the Isle of Man TT lost its Grand Prix status in 1976 and then the TT Formula One series lost world championship status after my second win in 1989, there was no real incentive for the short circuit riders to race there any more. And short-circuit racers are the most talented, which is not rocket science. For a good few years, the TT winners have come from riders who struggled at British Championship level on the short circuits. I was the last short-circuit specialist to win a TT race, although I think that will soon change. With the increased TV exposure there is more money in the sport again, and some of the better riders in the British Championship are starting to see the TT as a decent payday. Good superbike riders like Josh Brookes and Peter Hickman are now giving it a go and will push the road race specialists like John McGuinness, Ian Hutchinson and Michael Dunlop hard, even if they are all fully fit.

Josh and Peter will be two of the favourites to win in 2018, for sure. I remember speaking to Josh about it six or seven years ago, when he was first considering the TT. He told me he was worried that something out of his hands, like a mechanical problem, might cost him his life. Sure enough, a few years later and he was there, but he didn't go at it like a bull in a china shop. He learned the circuit over a number of years and gradually built up confidence, speed and courage. That's the right way to do it – it takes at least three years to learn the Isle of Man. If you go straight out there and try to ride the wheels off your bike, you are asking for trouble.

It worries me that some of the short-circuit riders are now tempted by the money, especially when they have young families. Okay, I did just that in 1992 when my daughter Danielle was very young, but I was at a stage in my career when I needed to fund my World Superbike career. The bikes are a lot faster now, too.

There is no doubt, though, that these men – and women – are wired differently. And for that reason, you will always have characters around. Anyone who starts being a prima donna in the TT paddock will be on the first ferry out of Douglas. The film *TT3D: Closer to the Edge* captured the heart of the soul of the TT brilliantly and made household names out of some of the riders, and rightly so. The year of filming, 2010, was perfect for the film's content, with great storylines like local lad Connor Cummings' spectacular crash over the side of the mountain, Ian Hutchinson's record-breaking five wins in the week, and Guy Martin's fireball crash into a stone wall at Ballagarey Corner from which he escaped with just a few broken vertebrae and a punctured lung.

The film launched Guy into the public eye. He's not the fastest rider in the world, but that doesn't make him a bad person, or a bad rider. He is quirky and has a distinctive look, and the public seem to love that. I don't know a lot about him, except that he likes a decent brew – and might have serviced a truck once or twice in his life. But I do know he is a very brave lad. Anyone who will strap himself into a box travelling at 400 mph across land or hurtle down a mountain on a tea tray or fly the fastest human-powered aircraft, as he did for his TV show *Speed*, deserves a lot of respect – and has a few screws loose!

Just like Guy, not a lot of people had heard about Hutchy before that film. But his performance that year puts him right up there with the greats of TT racing – five wins in a week in all the major races is incredible and will probably never be repeated. His story since that year is even more incredible and he has become one of my racing heroes. (It's just a shame he comes from the wrong side of the Pennines.)

Just a few weeks after his TT wins, Hutchy was involved in a horrible crash in atrocious conditions for a British Supersport round at Silverstone. Two bikes ran over his left leg and when he woke up in hospital he had to beg the surgeons not to amputate. It was touch and go for a while, but one of the three major blood vessels was still intact and basically kept his foot alive. I was watching the TT from Bray Hill the following year and found a spot at the front of the garden next to a softly-spoken lad on crutches, before I realised it was Ian. I knew from Twitter that he had been through some dark times.

'Chin up, lad, it could be worse – you could be dead,' I told him. The fans gave him a great reception when he rode a few parade laps that year, and a few months later, amazingly, on a modified bike with a right-hand gear shift and thumb brake, he came third in the Macau GP, a race which takes some balls when you are fully fit, believe me. But the bones hadn't healed properly and had become infected, so when he had a slight slip at a mini-bike slide demonstration at the London Bike Show at the start of 2012, his leg snapped again. Yet he somehow managed to race at the TT that year, before starting a gruelling 18-month road to recuperation to try and mend the leg properly with more operations, more pins and fixators, and more painful physio and training. It must have been torture for a lad who was determined to prove all the doctors wrong and win again. And that winning feeling returned in the Macau GP of 2013, well ahead of his scheduled return to racing.

I was really impressed that he returned to the short circuits in the British Superstock Championship to sharpen himself up for his road racing. And, man, was he sharp for 2015, almost equalling his record of five wins with three first places, second place in the Superbike race and third in the Senior. How the hell did he do that? This man had been to hell, slaved there for a while, escaped, been recaptured and then escaped again. A true *Miracle Man*, as his autobiography is called. The fact he didn't win BBC Sports Personality of the Year that year makes another mockery of the award.

It doesn't stop there, though. He won the two Supersport races again in 2016 to draw level with Mike Hailwood on 14 wins, and won the TT and Superstock races in 2017 before disaster struck, again. Dicing for the lead with Peter Hickman, his front tyre blew approaching the 27th marker, a fast-right kink. The crash fractured his left leg again and he was only just able to drag himself off the racing line before the next rider came through. That amazing resilience is still there, though, and let's hope he can climb to the top of the podium again one day. Even if he doesn't, I reckon he is the most amazing rider in the history of the TT and deserves every one of his trophies.

The same goes for the sidecars guys – I have a lot of respect for them. You can hear the sidecars half a mile off. Then, suddenly, it's there, skipping all over the road in a cloud of dust. I was once offered a go as the passenger by former world champion Steve Webster but told him to forget it. I'm not a good passenger at the best of times, even in a car. So the thought of putting my life in the hands of the driver of one of those things was a non-starter. Michaela, on the other hand, will give anything a go and was taken round Misano by Steve and loved it. Of course, Kev also wanted a turn, so Steve took him on a lap, too.

'Sidecars my arse,' Kev said, when he hopped out. 'I thought this was supposed to be a man's sport. I was asleep by the second bend.'

'Right, let's go round again,' said Steve. He actually meant two laps.

'I'll give you £100 if you can lose him in the gravel,' I laughed.

When they came back again Kev was nearly in tears, he could barely stand up, his leathers were soaking and he was as white as a sheet. Steve had been going so fast that Kev's helmet had been scraping on the track. At one point on the second lap, going into the chicane, Kev was so knackered that he thought about letting go and falling out deliberately. He apologised immediately for taking the piss. Needless to say, we were in stitches. I see Chris Walker has been having a go, but he knocked himself about badly last year. It might be time for him to come and do DirtQuake with me, instead.

But if the sidecar lads deserve their trophies, I can't say the same thing about the winner of the electric bike race. Joey Dunlop must be turning in his grave to see that one lap on a Hoover qualifies as a TT race victory. I have nothing against electric bikes in general. I understand that our planet has limited resources. But wouldn't it make more sense to put all our efforts into wind or hydro-electric power? Don't we have to build more garages, powered by fossil fuels, to run electric bikes and cars?

My other worry is that you can't hear electric vehicles coming, so is there not a safety issue? I think I will be long gone before electric bikes take over, but I don't think they will ever become a racing spectacle. You need noise in motorsport. Formula One tried to reduce the noise and look where that ended up – back at square one. And I don't think anyone would be kidded by artificial noise.

As for the best TT rider of all time? Joey? McGuinness? Neither, in my opinion. The fastest guy I have ever seen around the Isle of Man was Steve Hislop. He had the edge on me round there – and it's never easy for me to admit that. I was faster on the short circuits and would not have even classed Steve as a rival. At that time, my main rivals were James Whitham, Terry Rymer, Rob McElnea and John Reynolds. But Hizzy could have gone on to win TTs for the next 10 years if he had continued to race there.

John McGuinness was the best of his era, for sure. I remember standing on the scaffolding of our rented house when he first came through in the Senior race, dust flying everywhere as he used every inch of the road. He was on a mission and obviously not going home without a race win that week, probably because everyone had written him off. Before the race, one of my mates pulled McGuinness out for the sweepstake and then checked his odds. At 14–1, I would have put our house on him if I had seen how psyched up he was. Sure enough, John just pulled the pin and won comfortably. His autobiography is called *Built for Speed*, but to look at him he is anything but. He's more built for working on a farm and driving a tractor. He was built for speed that day, though. John's a likeable Lancashire lad – in fact, I can just about see his house from my bedroom on a clear day – never afraid to speak his mind and very single-minded. But I fear that his crash in the North West 200 last year, when he broke his leg badly as well as fracturing four vertebrae and three ribs, might mean that he doesn't add to his 23 race wins at the TT.

Michael Dunlop is another one-off, an animal on the bike. I remember him as an annoying little lad when I was racing against his dad, Robert, and I once visited their family home. It was a weird place, almost like a stately home but with sheep running around, shitting everywhere. Robert, who won five TTs, was killed in a crash during qualifying at the North West 200. Michael went out and won the 250cc race there just two days later. That takes something a bit special. He comes across as quiet and polite, but inside there must be an angry young man. That's how he looks on a bike – a force of nature. Michael will ride the wheels off any bike and has won three of the big races with different manufacturers – Honda, BMW and Suzuki – amongst his 15 TT victories.

Then, of course, there's Joey. With 26 wins, he is still the most success-ful TT rider of all time and I have many fond memories of Joey (not including the time I was carried out of his pub at 5 am in the morning after he introduced me to potato wine, or poteen, which is about 90 per cent proof). But it was his final appearance at the TT, in 2000, that I will remember the most. Bear in mind that his first win was in 1977. So to win the Formula One TT 23 years later at the age of 48 was incredible. There is no way your reactions are the same at that age. Your fitness is not as good for handling a 1000cc bike. And you wouldn't take the same chances. Not content with the Formula One win, Joey followed it up with two more wins in the 125 and 250 races. It was an amazing achievement.

I was recovering from my own career-ending crash at the time and remember thinking: 'For f**k's sake, Joey, just walk away and retire. You've achieved all you need to.' But racing was in his blood and he would prob-ably be racing classic bikes to this day. We all know what happened next. Just a few weeks later 'Yer Maun', one of the nicest blokes you could wish to meet and a real gentleman of racing, was killed at an obscure race in Estonia.

That's why I am uncomfortable with some of the riders taking on the most dangerous circuit in the world for too long. If you knock on the door too many times, somebody will answer. I was so upset when Karl Harris, who I liked a lot, lost his life in a crash on the mountain at Joey's Corner in the Superstock race in 2014. He had been British Supersport Champion three times and was coming to the end of a good career. He didn't need to start doing the TT at the age of 34, and I warned him about it. Even if you approach it sensibly, as Karl seemed to be doing, there's always the chance of a freak accident like that one. Then Shoey, who me and Whit crewed for that time, was killed two years ago at the age of 50. Especially when you have a young family, there has to be a time to call it a day. And I hate to say it, especially after his serious injury, but I would be happy to see John McGuinness call it a day now and enjoy his family, his health, his lifestyle. With his reputation and connections, he could run a race team if he wanted to stay involved in the sport.

Hey, even I had a go at that . . .

FOGGY PHENOMENA
10 motorbike characters

Marco Lucchinelli

A true rock 'n' roll star of our sport. Always makes me laugh.

James Whitham

My best mate in racing. Oh, and he could ride, too.

Joey Dunlop

Yer Maun. One of the nicest guys to talk to, if you could tell what he was saying.

Anthony Gobert

A talent gone to waste.

John Kocinski

A character indeed, but a very odd one at that.

Wayne Gardner

A big personality who rode with his heart, not necessarily his head.

Evil Knievel

Bit of a daredevil!

Anthony 'Slick' Bass

Larger-than-life guy who always, as my mechanic, put me first.

Alan Carter

Very handy with his fists, even with marshals who were trying to help him.

Steve Parrish

Never drop your guard for one second when Parrish is around.

7

SHY AND RETIRING

In some ways, I was lucky that the decision to retire was taken out of my hands – and very lucky to be here to tell the tale. I have no memory whatsoever of the actual crash at Phillip Island back in April 2000. Conditions for race one were wet and windy, but it looked like it would clear up and we switched from wets to intermediates at the last minute, as did the rest of the field – except for Anthony Gobert, who stuck with wets on his Bimota.

Anthony, or the Go Show, as he was nicknamed, was possibly the most talented rider I have ever seen on a motorcycle. He burst onto the scene in 1994 when he became the youngest rider to win a WSBK race at the age of 19. I met his dad that year and he took us out on his boat. Before he left the harbour, he was cracking open a few tinnies. His dad looked genuinely hurt when I told him I'd have a Diet Coke instead, so it wasn't difficult to see where the influence came from. You would often see

Anthony walking down the pit-lane with a beer in his hand straight after a practice session. Out on the track he was great to watch, backing it hard into the corners, but he was rarely going to be consistent over 25 laps because he didn't put the hard work in on Fridays and Saturdays.

I think he once pissed in Neil Hodgson's helmet after a race in Brno and Neil went mental. Later that night, he threw Anthony's Honda Cub into some bushes. Some lucky Czech guy must have one day found himself a nice little paddock bike.

Anthony won two more races in 1995 and then three in 1996, before signing for the factory Suzuki team in 500cc GPs. But he was kicked out of that team after a failed drugs test for marijuana and was then sacked again by the Ducati AMA team, after winning one more WSBK race as a wild card at Laguna Seca. The last I heard of him, he'd been in trouble with the cops in Australia for mugging an old lady. What a sad waste of talent.

Anyway, local knowledge worked for Gobert on this occasion and he cleared off to win the first race, while I was a comfortable second. It was dry for the afternoon race and after a bad start I was charging through the field. The next thing I knew, I could hear a helicopter. And I was on a stretcher, drifting in and out of consciousness. Then I was in a hospital bed with drips inserted everywhere and Michaela by my side.

To this day, I'm still not exactly sure what happened. The most accurate account came a few years later from a former racer from New Zealand, who saw everything. The bike of an Austrian rider, Robert Ulm, was misfiring and he pulled off the racing line in the fast section coming out of the Southern Loop. As he came back onto the racing line, I clipped him and flew into the tyre wall. No airbags, just a hard tyre wall. I bounced off and lay motionless. The Kiwi guy said everyone around feared the worst. But I had hit the tyre wall with my shoulder *and* head. It could have been so very different if it had been my head alone.

My humerus was fractured in three places near the shoulder joint and this was pinned back together in Australia. But while all the attention was on the recovery from my shoulder injury, not as much attention was paid to the severe concussion I suffered. For the next six months, I felt weak and sleepy. That whole period passed by in a bit of a blur.

The damage to the blood supply, nerves and tissue around the shoulder joint was worse than first feared and this was affecting how the bone was healing. Within a couple of months, I knew I would not race again that year. That alone was hard to enough to cope with. The bike was great, I was riding well and I had been confident another world title was there for the taking. Then I received another kick in the teeth when *Motor Cycle News* used the headline 'Who Needs Foggy?' on their front page after the Donington round of the championship in June, when Neil Hodgson and Chris Walker came first and second in the second race after Colin Edwards crashed and Frankie Chili's bike seized near the end. The headline was not meant to be hurtful, but it hurt all the same. After all, I'd been paraded around in the back of an open-topped car at Donington and virtually mobbed.

At Brands Hatch a month or so later, I tried a couple of demonstration laps but felt terrible on the bike, despite the amazing reaction from the crowd again. 'If it's this bad when I'm just wobbling round, what's it going to be like at speed,' I thought. There was only one way to see for sure and Ducati arranged a private test for me at Mugello in September. I managed just a couple of laps. I was in agony and couldn't even get down behind the screen. The decision was made for me. It was time to hang up my leathers. Perhaps people still do not realise the extent of that injury. If I had broken my neck, it might have been easier for some fans to accept my retirement. But even though a shoulder injury isn't as serious, the damage to the joint meant that I would never be able to wrestle a super-bike around those circuits at anything like top speed. And I wasn't about to make up the numbers.

The announcement was made on 21 September, a month after the launch of my autobiography. The reaction from the fans to the book was unbelievable. I think the publishers expected to sell around 20,000 copies. Eh? Had they not seen the crowds at Brands the previous year? Surely most of those fans would want a copy?

When I turned up for the first book signing, in the City of London, I could see a queue of people stretching around the corner and beyond.

'What's that for?' I asked the book's publicist, Jane Beaton.

'It's for your signing,' she said.

That signing lasted for three hours, and it was the same story all around the country. In Manchester, they needed mounted police to control the crowd and the chat-show event had to be switched to the cathedral at the last minute to accommodate everyone. Even in smaller places like Elles-mere Port, the fans turned out in force. The first print run of 30,000 sold out in two days and the book went on to sell over 250,000 copies, which blew the publisher's expectations out of the water.

It was the boost I needed at that time and helped take my mind off the fact that I wouldn't be racing again. But then came the backlash. I was a different person when I wrote that book – very self-centred and selfish. I was up my own arse and believed my own press. I had lost touch with good mates, who had stuck by me through thick and thin in the early days. The more I won, the more big-headed I became. It didn't matter to me if 20 per cent of the fans at Brands Hatch might have wanted me to crash and burn, as long as the other 80 per cent were right behind me. As far as I was concerned, that gave me licence to say what I wanted.

All that meant I was way too blunt in the book about people who really mattered to me. I pissed off my mum and my sister, and I really regret that now as it took a while for the dust to settle. That was the Foggy then. The Foggy now is a different person altogether. I am able to laugh at myself. I don't take life anywhere near as seriously. And I confront my demons head on.

Those demons are mental health issues – and I'm not afraid or embarrassed to admit that. A lot of people struggle to understand how someone with success, fame, money and a beautiful family can suffer from depression or anxiety. Especially when it's someone who was known for his mental toughness. But mental health is not about how much money there is in your bank account. It's not even about being tough. It's just something I can't control, although I have learned to deal with it.

I suffer a lot from anxiety and a lack of confidence. I can lie awake for hours ahead of a public appearance worrying about how many people will turn up or whether I will go down well. Then I wake up in the morning and think: 'What the hell was all that about?' At first, I used to fight it and tell myself to get a grip. But it's the depression or anxiety that gets a grip of you. Mental illness is complicated and can be caused by a number of factors such as family history, stress, medications and existing medical conditions that all affect how your brain controls your mood. This can cause a chemical imbalance and I tried the tablet route after discussing everything with my GP. But I must admit that I didn't read the box properly. It directed me to increase the dose after a couple of weeks and, after talking to a few mates who are also on anti-depressants, there is no chance of the pills working if you don't do that. After a couple of months, I stopped taking them altogether. I was sure that I was mentally tough enough to beat this thing on my own. Michaela felt I didn't have the patience to give them time to work. Sure enough, things didn't improve so I went back to the doctor about a year later and we tried a different medication. This made me tired during the day, so I stopped taking those, too. Medications might work for some people, but I don't like the idea of relying on pills for the rest of my life. My GP also recommended that I go to see some kind of counsellor, who would help me deal with attacks of depression or anxiety through breathing exercises or meditation techniques. Not for me. Again, I thought I was mentally strong enough to deal with it myself.

That mental toughness might even be part of the problem. When I was such a single-minded, headstrong racer, I had to have everything just as I wanted it. And I had people around me to make sure that happened. So perhaps it's harder for me to cope now, when something is not just as I want it. Maybe this is all just part of my make-up. Sure, I've chilled and mellowed a lot since my racing days, but I think that things get on top of you more and more as the years pass by.

I can be fine for weeks before something will set me off again. It might be something minor like one of the kids scratching their car, or there might be loads of food in the fridge about to go out of date. I can be irritated that there is so much stuff around the house that I never use, such as too much clutter in my garage. Trivial things can really wind me up. Then I start getting depressed about being so anxious. It's a vicious circle. Boredom doesn't help, either. I'm lucky that I am really busy most of the time but, if I do have too much time on my hands, that's usually when negative thoughts creep in. I also think it can be worse when I'm recovering after a few too many drinks. Some people drink to improve their mood, but I don't do that. I'm not the type to have a drink just because I've had a hard day. But we like to have a few beers or glasses of wine at the weekend and I can be down for the next couple of days when I'm tired. I've never been a big drinker, but I have definitely cut back over the last couple of years for that reason. Social media can be another trigger, too. I reckon it causes a lot of anxiety. You can't help reading stuff that winds you up and I reckon we were all a lot more relaxed before social media.

Having said all that, my mental health has definitely improved over the last couple of years, so maybe my approach of tackling it head on has worked to some extent. I still have the occasional bad day, though. I have learnt that one of the best things for me is to get out in the fresh air and either take the dogs for a walk along the river or get on my mountain bike. It really clears my head and helps me vent my frustrations, in much the same way I did when I was racing. Sure, that won't be for everyone, but I do recommend exercise outdoors as a way to cope for anyone who may be struggling.

The other thing I have learnt to do is to talk to someone, usually Michaela or perhaps Kev. They are always sympathetic and try to help, although I'm not sure I would be as useful if the shoe was on the other foot. It's like that scene from *Crocodile Dundee*, when the city woman tells Mick about one of her friends, who is seeing a psychiatrist.

'Hasn't she got any mates?' asks Mick.

'I suppose you don't have any shrinks in Walkabout Creek,' she answers.

'Nah,' says Mick. 'Back there, if you have a problem you tell Wally. And he tells everyone in town . . . brings it out in the open . . . no more problem.'

If someone approached me for help, I'd probably be more like Wally and pass it on to the lads I go trail-riding with. They'd take the piss with a few group WhatsApp messages and . . . no more problem. Seriously, though, just telling Michaela that today's not a good day can really help. It's much better when everything is out in the open. She'll ask if there's something getting me down and, most of the time, I can't put my finger on anything specific. That's when I realise again what a great life I actually do have.

So I encourage everyone who might be suffering with similar problems to talk to a family member, a friend, or a doctor. You will be surprised how many other people are suffering just like you. Also, if you know someone who might be having problems, don't be scared of asking them if they would like to talk. We all get down now and again, but not everyone realises the extent of their problems.

Depression is very common in sportsmen and sportswomen, especially straight after retirement. All of a sudden, their purpose has gone, and they feel isolated and frustrated. In some cases, they are no longer able to even participate in the sport that has dominated their life. And the depression I suffered soon after retirement was very different to the mental health problems I have now.

Perhaps it was just not being able to race any more. Perhaps I was bitter to see that the WSBK series had become so popular through Sky TV's coverage and my success and that I was no longer a part of it. Perhaps I was bitter seeing others sneak through the door that my retirement had left open. Perhaps it was a combination of all these factors. But I found I could not watch bike racing any more. I cancelled my subscription to *Motor Cycle News* – I could not bear to even read my own interviews. When I was racing, I was somebody and people were ready to listen, even if they didn't agree with me. Now that I was no longer racing, people seemed much more ready to shoot me down whenever I opened my mouth.

The thing that kept me going during that time was the fun I was having trail-riding with my mates like Kevin Moore, Mark Winstanley and Austin Clews, whose family owned CCM. The punters that came along were starting to see a different side to me, someone who was willing to let his hair down and have a bit of fun. CCM was also starting to run supermoto track days as well as the enduro ride-outs. It was a sport that was becoming really popular – a mix of dirt and tarmac sections in a flat-track short-circuit. Austin asked me to go down to one of their track days at the Three Sisters track near Wigan, but it wasn't too long after my accident and I was a bit wary of putting myself in a position where a crash was going to mess up my shoulder again. But I couldn't stand the thought of missing out on the fun, so I went down to see what all the fuss was about (Oh, and I just happened to have my leathers and helmet with me, of course!) CCM's British supermoto champion, Warren Steele, was also there practising.

'Don't go getting the red mist and chasing Warren,' said Kev. 'You've not been on a supermoto before. They take some getting used to.'

After three or four laps, I binned it and went sliding into the gravel. And, sure enough, the red mist came down. I got back on and people said my knee was down like I was riding a superbike at some corners – none of the leg-dangling we've already talked about. I managed to catch Warren, had a quick cheeky glance across at him, and cleared off, lapping about two seconds quicker.

Austin saw the potential and suggested I enter a big supermoto event in Mettet, Belgium, where I would be on a 700cc single-cylinder against some pretty handy riders on 450cc four-strokes. I could have had my arse kicked big time. Word got out that I was going to compete and one story suggested around 14,000 tickets had been sold to Brits who were travelling out to watch me. So we had to take this seriously and CCM put in a lot of work on setting the bike up for me.

I wanted as much time on the bike as possible and enjoyed riding it on the roads on the moors around Darwen or Bolton on a Sunday with a few of the lads. One afternoon that summer, we came across a bunch of lads out on their Fireblades and R1s at a busy crossroads. Each of them had their girlfriend on the back on a seat the size of a playing card. I was wearing an open-faced helmet and took off my goggles to wipe them when I stopped at the junction. The bloke next to me did a double take and screamed 'F**kin' 'ell, it's Foggy!' When there was a gap in the traffic I pulled away, in an orderly manner of course, and let's just say my bike was a bit better suited to the tight twisty roads than their superbikes. I looked around a couple of times and couldn't see anyone, even our guys. A few miles down the road, I pulled in to let my mates catch up. Kev turned up, crying with laughter and barely able to keep his bike upright.

'You should have seen the carnage you caused back there,' he wheezed. 'Those guys thought they were racing you at Brands Hatch and totally forgot about their girlfriends. It was pandemonium. I saw backsides a foot in the air, bikes totally on the wrong side of the road. One guy ended up in a farmer's drive. Every single girl was in tears.' Then, right on cue, one of them rolled up with weeds and heather in his fairings, and his girlfriend as white as a sheet.

As part of the preparation for Belgium, they booked the circuit at Anglesey for a private track day for me on 21 September, a year to the day after my retirement. Straightaway I was faster than the pace at the British Championship round the previous week.

Maybe I was going a bit too fast. On a gravel section, in fourth gear and sliding round a left turn back onto the tarmac, I hit the back brake and thought: 'I've got this all wrong.' The bike threw me up and over and I was heading for the banking. Instead of relaxing, like I did for that famous 'air walk' crash at Sugo in 1995, I tensed and stuck my leg out. It hit the banking and snapped like a dry twig. Badly. The first thought was the same as always – she's going to kill me. Michaela was at that very moment handing over my credit card to pay for a new dress for a night out with James and Andrea Whitham which we had planned that evening in Manchester. The dress ended up on the floor as she stormed out of the shop when she got the call.

My next thought was: 'I'm in the middle of nowhere here.' It took an age for the ambulance to turn up and take me to Bangor Hospital on the bumpiest roads imaginable, jarring the jagged edges of the fractures with every jolt. Perhaps a bit muddled by the gas and air, I was hoping the doctors might be able to cast it quickly so that I could be out in time for the restaurant booking in Manchester. It took Michaela a couple of hours to drive down, but that wasn't long enough for her to have calmed down.

'You f**king idiot, you were supposed to be retired from all this,' she yelled, bursting into the hospital room. 'Nurse,' I shouted, pressing the panic button. 'Get this mad woman out of my room. I don't feel safe.' Michaela stormed out and was heading back north before she decided to stop in a hotel on the way home and return the next morning, ever so slightly apologetic.

It proved to be a long recovery. The gaps between the bones didn't heal properly initially and some bone was grafted from my hip to pack into the space. A plate was pinned over the fracture and removed 18 months later. It's never a good time for this kind of thing to happen, but this was especially bad timing because I was really struggling with the ambassador role that I had agreed with Ducati. So far, I had been wheeled out at a crappy little show in Germany and a Ducati Ladies Day at Oulton Park. It wasn't me. My head was not in the right place to be around people who wanted to ask me all about my racing days. It's so different now in my ambassadorial role for Triumph, which I really enjoy. Again, I think people can see now that I have a lot more time and appreciation of the fans.

Only two weeks before the supermoto crash, Ducati had asked me to attend the World Superbike round at Assen. It was torture. This was the circuit I could call my own, with 12 wins from my 14 appearances there. Now I had to watch Troy Bayliss, who took my place at Ducati after my injury, win both races with the help of team orders in the second race. My team-mate from the previous year, Ruben Xaus, allowed Bayliss to pass and secure the world title. Ruben set the fastest lap of the weekend – half a second slower than my 1999 lap record.

'This is shit,' I thought. 'It's too soon – I'm not ready for this. It's all too raw.'

The best place for me to escape from it all was a holiday home we then owned in Jávea, Spain. It was there, while lying on a sun lounger, that I received a timely call.

'Carl, remember me? This is David Wong in Malaysia . . .'

8

BAT OUT OF KL

I first received a call from David Wong out of the blue in 1992 telling me that he ran a team for Petronas, Malaysia's oil and gas company, in the Malaysian Superbike Championship and their results were not up to scratch. He'd heard on the grapevine that I was running as a privateer that year and wanted me for their final three races. I could have done without the distraction so quoted a fee that I thought would put him off – £3,000 per race plus business-class flights and expenses. He accepted straight-away. This was obviously a guy with deep pockets. He also offered to buy my Ducati at the end of the season.

David met me in Singapore, where he lived, because the first race was in Johor, just over the bridge connecting Singapore to Malaysia. He knew how to look after his guests and we hit it off instantly. 'You win races for this crazy Chinaman, right?' he chuckled. I won the first two races and the bike broke down in the third, but David was chuffed and was as good as his word to buy the Ducati. We stayed in touch for many years, until his sad death in 2016, and David often came to watch me whenever I raced in places like Indonesia. He was a man who touched the hearts of a lot of people in motorsports.

Wind the clock forward to 2001 and I knew that David meant business when he started rabbiting on about an exciting project he wanted to discuss. Word had reached him that I was looking for sponsors to run my own Ducati team in World Superbikes. It was something that had been proposed to me by a few guys who were involved with one of my sponsors at the start of 2000, a website company called Bikes4U. One of them was an impressive guy called Murray Treece, who had a background in technology company start-ups. The idea appealed to me because, if I wasn't able to race myself, at least I could win again as a team owner. It would have meant I had a purpose in the sport again, and more than just being rolled out to smile in front of the cameras and fans. But, until we found some hard cash, I wasn't getting too excited about it. I didn't really understand what David was proposing – something about running a team with a new bike that Petronas were developing with Sauber, the Formula One engine guys. Their brand-new engine had been revealed at the Japanese GP in March. 'What's this got to do with superbikes?' I thought. So I asked my manager, Neil, to give David a call.

'There's definitely something in this,' he told me after speaking to David. Petronas had developed a 900cc triple engine with the intention of going to GPs in 2003, when the new MotoGP rules would allow four-strokes – in direct competition with World Superbikes. The triple was seen to be the best of both worlds, so you got the power delivery of a twin and the grunt of a four-stroke. But when David heard about my plans for Team Foggy Racing, a new company we set up to explore the idea of me running a team, his business instincts kicked in. What if Petronas used the engine to build a bike for World Superbikes? Because superbikes is a production series, there would have to be a minimum number of bikes on sale to the public. And Petronas, which is owned and run by the Malaysian government, could then use these bikes to kick-start the Malaysian motorbike industry as a manufacturer in their own right. It all started to make sense.

'David wants to fly us over to Kuala Lumpur to see if we can make it work,' Neil said. 'But me and you can't talk to them about the technical stuff. We should involve Murray.'

By the time a date was set for the meeting, I was in a cast from my supermoto accident, so there was no way I could fly out to Malaysia, which I was a bit gutted about, although I had full confidence in Neil and Murray, who were like kids in a sweetshop when they returned from their flying visit.

'Look, Carl, this could be huge,' said Neil. 'Petronas are talking about a five-year sponsorship deal worth tens of millions and building a bike with your name on it. This could be a game-changer.'

I have never been a risk-taker in business, which might seem strange for someone who risked his life as a career. Me and Michaela always preferred to invest our money in low-to-medium risk options rather than chasing big returns from risky ventures. But this deal did seem too good to be true – it wasn't going to cost us a penny and had huge long-term potential. Still, it was a massive leap of faith for me. My deal with Ducati wasn't to be sniffed at. I had turned my back on them once and look where that got me. And I had this niggling doubt about adapting a brand-new engine for World Superbikes. Could we really pull this off?

Murray started working on a business plan for the race team and Petronas asked an English company, MSX, to develop a business plan for building the 150 bikes that would be needed to meet the World Superbike homologation rules. And before we knew it Murray and Neil were back in Malaysia to try to seal the deal. Just like the last trip, they planned to stay overnight and return the next day. They eventually came back two weeks later after some tough negotiations.

Although Petronas is a huge company, they spend their money wisely. We had to justify every dollar and present a strong case for the benefits of sponsoring the team. It was also tough for me, stuck back in England and fretting whether to throw myself into this crazy project with crazy deadlines. Petronas wanted to be racing the very next season, but we didn't even have a drawing of a bike. We did have a name for it, though – the FP1, the F standing for Fogarty and P for Petronas. And the team would be called Foggy Petronas Racing, FPR. The agreement was in place, but Petronas were taking my delay as a bit of an insult to their integrity, plus we were wasting valuable time for the project. I had to take the plunge.

After some last-minute wrangling, we came away with a budget of $39 million to set up the team and run the FP1 in World Superbikes for five years. It was a healthy budget, but FPR was starting with literally nothing. We needed premises, staff, trucks, hospitality, riders ... prayers. Oh yes, and a bike. Don't forget the bike. Even starting from a blank piece of paper, I thought we might just be able to have a bike ready for our planned start date of July at Laguna Seca. It was against all the odds, but it was just about possible. Our main problem was the parallel road bike programme. How on earth were we going to be able to build a race bike in that time, knowing it had to be mass-produced? That kind of project took five years of planning, not five months. We needed 75 road-going FP1s ready in time to race. Really?

It didn't help when Sauber quickly decided they wanted no part of the superbike project, which was called Project Misty within Petronas. Project Foggy might have been more accurate. Sauber's intention had been to commercialise the engine in MotoGP, but there were suggestions that they had priced themselves out of the market, causing Petronas to go back to the drawing board and go down the superbike path. Their departure was not a disappointment for us, because we wanted to work with a British engine developer like Cosworth or Ricardo. So, when we were told that the development of the engine had been handed to Eskil Suter, a Swiss former racer who had set up a business specialising in developing clutches, there was a lot of scratching of heads and gnashing of teeth. I assumed Petronas must have known something that we didn't. To the best of our knowledge Suter, who was obviously a very clever guy, had never developed an engine in his life. Why take the chance on someone unproven in a project like this? If the bike didn't perform well, all this money would be wasted.

Then I needed a strong backbone of people to help me make the transition from rider to team owner. This picked itself, really. Nigel Bosworth, a good mate from my racing days who went on to manage the Red Bull Ducati team, was already lined up as team manager. Murray had the business brains and was appointed Chief Executive Officer, Neil was in charge of marketing, and my long-term financial adviser, Martin Williams, controlled the purse-strings. Me and Michaela made up the board.

There was a steep cultural learning curve, too. Malaysia is a devout Muslim nation and there is a different way of doing things over there, as I discovered on my first trip out to meet our new partners. I was a bit nervous walking into Petronas' Twin Towers in KL. It's one of the tallest buildings in the world and definitely one of the most impressive.

When we walked into the huge reception area, you could hear a pin drop. Every step echoed all around us. All the staff were going about their business in silence, and security was really tight. Neil and Murray had been lecturing me for days about all the things I should and shouldn't do or say, in case I caused offence. So all this stuff was going through my head as we queued in silence to hand our passports in at reception.

All of a sudden, Neil let out this almighty scream in his numpty Northern accent: 'F**kin' 'ell!' That scared me and I turned to see a huge black thing the size of a fruit bat taking off while Neil tried to batter it with his briefcase. It was actually a huge black butterfly that had been camouflaged until Neil bent down to pick up his bag. His expletives were still echoing their way up each of the 84 floors up to the top of the building. 'F**kin' 'ell . . . F**kin' 'ell . . . F**kin' 'ell . . . F**kin' 'ell . . .' Devout Muslims, who had never heard such foul language in their lives, were covering their ears and saying prayers. Some were hiding under their desks, thinking there was some kind of attack going on. Neil was sweating buckets and looked like he was about to have a heart attack. And I was rolling around the marble floor in hysterics. Murray had a face like thunder. 'Get a grip,' he growled, which made it even funnier to me. I hadn't recovered by the time we made it up to the Motorsports Division on the 71st floor. It's a weird sensation up there. You can feel the building swaying slightly when it's windy. And when the heavens open at about 4pm every day, which you can set your watch by, you can sometimes be above the clouds looking down on the storm below.

Every so often during that meeting, when I was being introduced to their top brass and should have been making a good impression, the butterfly incident came back to me and I burst into giggles. That set Neil off, too. And Murray's face grew angrier and angrier. We had just about composed ourselves when it was time to go out for dinner, at a special street entertainment event that Petronas had laid on. There was a huge spread of food already on the table and I dived in. After hoovering down about 10 chicken skewers like Homer Simpson, I looked up, with satay sauce dribbling down my chin, and everyone was staring at me in stunned silence. Nobody else had touched their food and Neil was mouthing at me to stop eating. I'd forgotten that it was Ramadan and it was forbidden to eat or drink until sunset. I was about an hour early. I apologised, but one of the Petronas guys said: 'Don't worry about it, it's not your religion.'

Back in England, we found an amazing unit near Burton-on-Trent and built offices, a storeroom, a dyno and a huge work space which included prayer rooms for the Muslim technicians that Petronas provided as part of the sponsorship package. We started work on a state-of-the-art hospitality set-up, which would not have been out of place in the Formula One paddock. Everything was branded in the Petronas colours, a turquoise-green, which wasn't the easiest to work with, but a guy called Michael Fisher from a company called Linney Design did a great job. We were going to look the bollocks. But even at that early stage, I was worried about how much we were spending. I felt I was railroaded into that by Murray and Neil. Of course, we needed to create a good impression for Petronas, but the best way of making a good impression was by winning races. And we still didn't have a bike.

While the engine was out of my control, I did have a big input on the look of the FP1. I knew exactly what I wanted and was involved in the very early drawings and clay-modelling. The chassis was based on a 500 GP design and I wanted it to look sexy, like a Ducati 916 and not like a Fireblade. It was also my idea to have the three exhaust pipes coming out under the seat. It looked fantastic but, when the bike finally came together, you couldn't sit on the seat for more than five minutes due to problems dispersing the heat.

The next few months were a whirlwind of activity, trying to pull everything together in time. The project was announced at the Bologna Bike Show in December, where we had our first meeting with our number one rider target, Troy Corser, my old team-mate. At first, I didn't dream we would be able to attract a rider of Troy's quality. I had already spoken with another old rival, Steve Hislop. It seemed that Hizzy was getting faster and faster on short circuits as his career went on and he'd been challenging for the British Championship in 2001 before breaking his leg badly at the penultimate round at Rockingham. I called him up and he was definitely interested, but a few weeks later I picked up *Motor Cycle News* to read he had signed for MonsterMob Ducati. He went on to win the British title in 2002 and then tragically lost his life in a helicopter crash the following year. Despite our rivalry in those early days at the TT, I always had a lot of time for Steve – he was a guest at our wedding – and I was devastated when I heard the news of his death.

I also approached another old rival, Simon Crafar, who, like Hizzy, was very fast on his day but perhaps struggled to ride round problems when things were not going his way. But when it became clear that Troy had missed out on the rider merry-go-round at the end of 2001, after not quite gelling with the Aprilia, he was the obvious choice. There was no doubting Troy's talent. He was the youngest winner of the World Superbike Championship at that time and was also really good at setting a bike up – something we would need in buckets. First, there were a couple of hurdles to overcome. Our riders would have to sit out the first half of the season before our first race at Laguna Seca. Although there would be lots of testing, that's no substitute for a racer in the prime of his career. And how were we going to afford him? Most of our Year 1 budget was being spent on the team infrastructure, so we didn't have a lot left for a big-name rider. Cash-flow wouldn't be such an issue for the following years, so we made him a three-year offer with a very tempting salary in Year 3 if he stuck it out.

I also wanted a British rider, someone I could nurture a little bit but also someone to fly the flag. I had noticed James Haydon in the British Championship as a very fast young lad on his day, who was often on the podium or just outside the top three and finished ahead of his Virgin Yamaha team-mate, Michael Rutter, in the final championship standings. Okay, he crashed a few times, but the fact that he was pushing it to the limit wasn't going to put me off. And he was as keen as mustard.

The riders were announced in January 2002, but then deadline after deadline was missed. It was really frustrating having to wait for decisions from Petronas because everything was linked into the road bike programme. It soon became clear that we didn't have a cat in hell's chance of racing at Laguna and I wasn't relishing the calls to the riders. Troy took it in his stride, he's a laidback kind of guy. But James was still making his name in the sport and was devastated. I couldn't even let him go and ride for someone else for half a season, because he was under contract.

The bikes were finally unveiled at a launch party in London in June 2002 and the press loved them. Now all we needed to do was fire up the engine. And that's when the real problems started.

FOGGY PHENOMENA
10 bikes

My Honda 50cc monkey bike

It all started here.

Ducati 916

An iconic bike, ahead of its time in looks and great to ride.

Honda RC30

Looked stunning and engine was bulletproof, but front end so hard to handle.

Honda 6

Hailwood's iconic bike. Outrageous. Unbelievable sound. What were Honda thinking of!?

MV Agusta 500

Agostini's bike that dominated the 1960s and 70s. Cool silver and red colours.

Triumph Thruxton

A classic bike brought into the modern era. Smooth handling and loads of torque.

Yamaha TZ250

Great times on this bike in the mid-1980s.

Suzuki RG500

Sheene's bike that killed off four-strokes. Changed the face of racing.

Yamaha OW01

A weapon of a two-stroke made famous by big names like Kenny Roberts, Freddie Spencer and Gene Romero.

FP1

Looked and sounded great but didn't go very fast or far.

9

FLAMIN' HELL

The first time the FP1 was run in public was as part of the 2002 Manchester Commonwealth Games torch relay. To say it was a PR gamble is an understatement. The bike had only done a few straight-line tests at Bruntingthorpe Aerodrome, and already it was obvious that the engine had some real problems, especially with leaking oil and overheating. I had been asked by the Commonwealth Games organisers to carry the torch on a motorbike and I couldn't very well ride a Ducati any more, so we bit the bullet and agreed that I would ride the FP1. I could just imagine the headlines if the bike broke down and the whole torch relay was ruined. Just about the only thing we could guarantee was keeping the torch alight, because one of the big issues was four-foot flames shooting out of the exhaust due to excess fuel burning off.

Thankfully, the bike behaved over my leg of the relay, a couple of miles of roads up on the Lancashire moors, and I couldn't believe the number of people who turned out so early in the morning. But that was nothing compared to the reception we received at Brands Hatch four days later at the WSBK round. The plan was for me and both riders to do a few demonstration laps before the final Superbike race, but a bad crash in the Supersport race put everything back and it all became really rushed. When Troy and James came back into the pits after their laps, the numbers on one of the bikes were quickly changed to my number 1 and, hearts in mouths, we fired up the bike again in the pit-lane. I managed to splutter round for a couple of laps, the bike misfiring all the way. 'For f**k's sake, don't cut out now,' I thought. It finally cut out coming into the pit-lane, but I made it back to our garage, my arse just about on fire from the heat under the seat. The massive crowd had gone mental and that was the boost the whole team needed.

My next challenge was getting home. That nasty Supersport crash involved – you guessed it – a certain Mr Whitham. He high-sided coming onto the start-finish straight and nearly flew straight into the pit wall. But he was up and about within an hour and the circuit doctors gave him the all-clear to travel home. Even so, he was shaken up, so I said he could use my mate's helicopter that was waiting for me and I would drive his van back. As usual after Brands the traffic was horrendous, and we were queued for over an hour at the Dartford Tunnel, so I rang James to see how he was.

'I'm grand,' he said. 'Just having a beer and a Chinese in the back garden. Only took 45 minutes to get home. Thanks, by the way.' I was spewing.

James does seem to have that knack of bouncing back from crashes. But not always. I remember being on holiday in Ibiza in 1999 when he was riding for Kenny Roberts' Modenas GP team at Brno. I went to watch the race in a beach bar and, true to form, within a few corners of the first lap James had crashed. His bike exploded and almost set the whole circuit on fire. I looked around at everyone in the bar to see if anyone could speak English.

'My amigo,' I pointed. 'El dickhead.' Nobody took much notice.

I went back to the beach and told Michaela. 'Guess what? James has crashed and most of the Czech Republic is on fire. And he's pretending he's hurt.'

That's something you should never say after a bike crash and I apologised to James later. He was in a bad way with a smashed pelvis and needed an operation in the local hospital. When he came around, he realised there was a catheter stuck up his cock – and he was thankful that he was under anaesthetic when it went up. After travelling home on a private Lear jet that was covered by his insurance, when it was time to leave Leeds Hospital the catheter had to come out. Along came a willing student nurse and gave the tube a little tug. Nothing doing. 'Bit 'arder, luv?' she asked. James nodded reluctantly. Still nothing doing. After a few more attempts, she had one leg on the bed and was heaving like the anchor man of a tug of war team. James' cock was now 12 inches longer, making a total of 15 inches, and 2 mm thick. He was in agony. One of the senior nurses heard the screams and asked whether the student had deflated the tube first. D'oh. She flicked a switch and eased the catheter out, much to James' relief.

After Brands the hard work started, as we tried to get the bike ready for the first race of the 2003 season. If we were not already up against it, there was another kick in the teeth when the FIM, the sport's governing body, changed the rules to allow 1000cc capacity across twins, triples and even four-cylinder bikes. We were suddenly 100cc down on the other manufacturers and all the advantages that we thought we would have as a triple were out the window. Thanks, guys, we really needed that. The only saving grace was that most of the Japanese manufacturers had turned their attentions to MotoGP, so this was probably the weakest the championship had ever been. A few of the big-name riders, like Troy Bayliss, Colin Edwards and Nori Haga, had also left for MotoGP.

Right from the start of the project, there had been a lot of whispers about whether the homologation rules were being bent to allow us into the championship. The plan was always to assemble the first 75 bikes, necessary to meet the first homologation target, in the UK and then move manufacturing to Malaysia. Once the next 75 bikes were built, those first 150 homologation specials would be sold at around £25,000, with the price coming down when high-volume production kicked in. *Motor Cycle News* published one cartoon by Sprocket showing a couple of bikes being inspected by the FIM in a factory with mirrors on the walls, which made it look like there were 75. Even if we had been allowed to cut corners by the FIM, we would not have been allowed by Petronas. That's not their way of doing things. Integrity is everything for them.

At the first track outing of the bike at Donington, we managed to get in the 1:38 s straight out of the box, which I thought was pretty impressive. Then we tested at Almeria, Lausitzring, Misano and Phillip Island, where Troy was within a second of the lap record, plus Sepang, where I rode the bike in anger for the first time. It felt really alien, especially on a circuit that I didn't know, with a completely different power band to what I was used to – much more like a two-stroke, with nothing much at the bottom end. The bike was capable of reasonable lap times, but reliability was already the main problem, and relations with Eskil Suter were strained right from the word go. We occasionally had to resort to quick fixes like Aralditing the crank cases to stop the oil leaks. Our big race debut at Valencia at the start of the 2003 season was heading for disaster.

Then Troy only went and stuck the thing on the front row.

We couldn't believe it. We all knew Troy was a Superpole specialist and capable of doing a fast lap around any circuit. And Valencia, a tight and twisty circuit with relatively short straights, suited a bike that was down on power. The FP1 handled well, as slower bikes do. Our problem would come in the races when we didn't have the power to overtake and were sitting ducks for the faster bikes down the straights. Still, to go from a blank piece of paper to a front-row start for a brand-new make of bike in just over 15 months was some going. For us, it was reason to celebrate. Perhaps a little too hard.

I don't think anyone could believe it. It had been a mental year and it was like a weight was lifted off our shoulders. So, while the mechanics worked long into the night getting the bikes prepped for race day, the team management and a good few people connected with the project went a bit nuts back at the team hotel. Troy had stayed back at the circuit to run through all the data with his crew chief and was a bit surprised to find us partying like we had won the world title when he got back to the hotel. There may have been a few raised eyebrows from some of the Petronas delegation, who were all non-drinkers, too.

There was less reason to celebrate on the Sunday. Troy crashed in the first race but was battling for fifth in the second race before settling for seventh place. James scored the first points for us with a twelfth place in the first race but retired with some technical issue on the ninth lap of race two. Our chief engineer, Steve Thompson, summed it up by saying: 'Never has so much effort gone into a seventh place in the history of bike racing.' And Troy also hit the nail on the head: 'We might not have set the world alight, but we certainly warmed it up.' Literally. The flames from the back of the FP1 were spectacular. Other riders were coming in at the end of the race with blistered fairings and melted visors. But the fans loved those flames and we built them into our merchandise designs and branding.

Things went downhill for the rest of the year. In the first nine rounds, we had something like 17 DNFs. At Brands Hatch, our home round, our best finish was seventeenth by James. Then Petronas slapped us with a fine when we only fielded Troy for the Silverstone round because James was out of action with a prolapsed disc in his neck, following a crash at Oschersleben. He had already been riding with a broken foot and shoulder and knee ligament damage from a crash at the previous round in Monza. In Germany, his bike jumped out of gear and he flew into the gravel at over 100 mph. Our thinking at the time was that, until the reliability issues were resolved, why risk another rider who was not used to riding the bike? As a result of that fine, money was even tighter, so I opted for an unknown local rider to replace James at the following round in Misano. Lorenzo Mauri, who was racing in the Italian Superstock Championship, was recommended by my old Ducati boss, Davide Tardozzi. The lad would have nothing to lose and everything to gain. By the end of the first day, he was in hospital with a badly broken leg. I felt terrible and regret that I didn't visit him in hospital.

I was already struggling by this point. This was all happening at the wrong time for me. I was still out of love with racing and I really didn't want to be around it. Plus I was frustrated with the delays, the technical problems and the in-fighting within the team. This project had my name on it, but I felt sidelined. I hated the board meetings, when it seemed I had no choice in any of the decisions. We also had a TV crew following our every move for a series called *Against All Odds* on the Men and Motors channel. The board meetings might have come across on TV as a barrel of laughs, but they were no laughing matter when the cameras were absent. It was a real struggle for me to put a brave face on things for the public and press. If the same opportunity came along today, I would be much more hands on. And I would be in a better place to manage the ups and downs of such a challenging project.

The one thing that kept me going was knowing that Petronas were in this for the long haul. The road bike was launched before the Malaysian MotoGP at the Twin Towers in October 2003, with an announcement of plans to build thousands of FP1s in Malaysia. This was a massive commitment for them – and I felt I had a duty to repay their good faith and generosity. There was a glimmer of hope on the horizon, too. It had been accepted that we needed a change of direction with the engine and Ricardo, one of our original preferences, were chosen to take over from Suter.

It was no surprise to anyone, least of all James himself, when I decided to replace him for 2004. In fact, I think he was probably relieved. He struggled on the bike more than Troy, for sure, but that was only to be expected. Troy was a lot more experienced. Realising he wasn't going to win races, Troy probably rode a bit within himself. I liked James, and still enjoy his company, but I wanted someone who was going to give Troy a run for his money. Luckily for me, English fans' favourite Chris 'Stalker' Walker was coming out of a lean year on the Kawasaki and was without a ride. I knew he would always give 100 per cent and bring that element of competition which you always want between your riders.

But first I had another difficult issue to deal with. I was hearing more and more grumbles about 'Boz', our team manager Nigel Bosworth. And it was coming from the very guys he had brought into the team, such as chief mechanic Steve Thompson and some of the other engineers. At first, I put that down to just the normal bitching and moaning that goes with any job. In fact, one thing the whole experience taught me was never to run a business. Back in my dad's day, you told an employee what to do and they got on with it or they were out on their ear. Now it's health and safety this, job description that, insurance, pensions – the list is endless. Basically, everyone wants to do as little as possible for as much money as possible. It's virtually impossible to get rid of anyone nowadays. How someone like Richard Branson sleeps at night I have no idea. When I heard that the rest of the management team were struggling with Boz, too, I felt backed into a corner and there was really only one option. He had to go. It was a tough call – this was an old friend and someone who was a key man in pulling the project together. But I knew I would have to be the one to break it to him.

The three of us sat down in Murray's office and I spelled it out. Boz was devastated and pleaded that he would try to put things right. I looked over at Murray, hoping there might be a way to avoid this. But Murray just shook his head. So that was that. Boz had to leave the premises there and then, because of the sensitivity of some of the information he had access to. He passed Chris Walker, who had just arrived to sign his contract, coming up the stairs. Chris must have wondered what on earth he'd let himself in for. That's another of the things I really regret about the whole FPR project. I shouldn't have bowed to the pressure and let Boz go.

After another busy winter of testing, it looked like all the hard work was starting to pay off. Conditions for the first race of the season were slightly damp, perfect for our bike as it made it more of a level playing field. Troy was actually dicing for the lead early on but crashed, probably trying too hard to seize this chance of a good result. Chris was running fourth with a few laps to go when Steve Martin crashed after his bike started spewing oil. 'We're third. We're only on for a f**king podium,' I thought. It was the longest three laps of my life – way too much for me to handle as a team owner. At least as a rider you have more control of the situation. I could see Chris approaching the final few turns and I stood on the pit-wall to cheer him in. But the emotions got the better of me and I jumped off onto the track as he came onto the start-finish straight. I nearly broke my bloody ankle – it was much higher than I thought. It also earned me a bollocking from the FIM. I thought those days were behind me! The first text I received was from Boz, congratulating the team on a job well done. Now that's character.

Next stop, Borneo. No, not Brno, Borneo. Every year, Petronas put on a massive street demonstration by their motorsports teams and this year it was in the city of Kuching, the capital of the state of Sarawak in the Malaysian part of Borneo. We were obviously on a bit of a high after the result in Valencia and we were in Petronas' good books. It was one big happy family. Before the big street demo, we visited local schools and everyone really enjoyed interacting with the kids in games and challenges. One challenge was to see how long someone could balance a BMX on one wheel and the Formula One team, including their driver Felipe Massa, were gobsmacked by Troy's balance. He could have stayed there all day if it hadn't been the hottest place on the planet. The crowds for the main event were incredible, too. I had never seen anything like it and it really rammed home how important Petronas is in Malaysia. We visited traditional longhouses, where a whole tribe lives under one roof, learned about the headhunting tribes, tried traditional blow-darts for hunting and visited the massive Petronas facilities. I'm not usually into all that stuff, but I really enjoyed the whole trip. It was a good chance to bond with Chris Walker, too. We were like a couple of giggling schoolkids on the back seat of the bus and, at the end of the trip, Murray suggested it was time to stop being his best mate and start becoming his boss. He had a point.

Perhaps Troy sensed a bit of favouritism, too, but it might just have fired him up a bit. At the third round of the championship, at Misano, Troy achieved the best result of our four years of racing with a second place. Again, the conditions were mixed and Troy led for most of the race before the French rider, Regis Laconi, came flying past just three laps before the race was stopped because of the rain. If it had rained a few minutes earlier, Troy would have won. But hang on a minute – we were sitting second in the manufacturers' standings and we had two podiums in three rounds. I'd thought it would have been good going to be on the podium by the end of the season. And, supposedly, there were significant engine developments just around the corner.

Misano was actually always one of my favourite rounds when I was racing. We stayed right on the beach at Hotel Kursaal, next to the main square in the nearby resort of Cattólica, so when business was finished at the circuit this was a great spot to kick back and relax. Some of my mates, including Kev and Mark, had started coming to a few rounds. This bunch of hooligans were up for a laugh at the best of times, so imagine what they were like when we actually had something to celebrate like that second place.

The drinks started to flow during dinner in the main square, which quickly fills up with locals enjoying some quiet family time. Not this night, though. Mark kicked it off with one of his favourite pranks – a 20 euro note tied to some fishing line, which was almost invisible. He would put this down about 10 or 15 yards from the table and wait for someone to try and pick it up. Then he would give the line a little tug just as the person was bending down. When we burst out laughing, most people realised what was going on and took it well. But the third or fourth guy who came along couldn't work out what was going on. Every time he bent down, Mark yanked the note a couple of feet nearer to our table and, after about five unsuccessful grabs, the bloke was virtually nose-to-nose with Mark when he slowly looked up and realised he'd been had. He was not amused and spat in Mark's face. Big mistake. Mark grabbed him by the throat and would have hurled him over the hotel into the sea like the Hulk if I hadn't thrown my beer over the guy and told him to f**k off. Not put off, Mark reeled in a few more victims, until one young guy was quick enough to stamp on the note, put it in his pocket and coolly wander off. Mark used a 5 euro note from then on.

Then someone bet Kev that he wouldn't run around the fountain in the main square stark bollock naked. What a waste of money. Kev didn't need any second invitation, whipped off his clothes and sprinted round, his hands covering his shame. Italian families with young kids, probably used to the behaviour of Brits abroad, just carried on with their meals without batting an eyelid. But Kev had made a schoolboy error and left his clothes at the table. So, by the time he got back, Mark had hurled them on top of a bus shelter and Kev had to climb onto the roof like a rat up a drainpipe, bollocks dangling down everywhere for all to see – including two passing policemen. They wandered calmly over and saw Kev on top of the bus shelter, scrambling to put his clothes back on. The coppers just shook their heads in dismay and left to see to more important business.

The next race was not for another month, so time for us to recover and fit in another team PR trip. This time it was to Shanghai, where Petronas was launching a new oil product at a round of the German Touring Car Championship, which held events in lots of different countries. But one journey halfway around the world to Borneo was enough for me. I was due to fly out to meet the team just before the Shanghai event, but persuaded Michaela to ring Neil with a cock-and-bull story about a jet-ski accident in 10-foot waves.

'He's in a bad way,' she said. 'He got a jump all wrong and smacked his head against the jet-ski. There's no way he can travel out there.'

He believed every word she said – and then he sent it out as a press release. The next day it was on the front page of the *Daily Star*, who made it sound like I was at death's door. Apparently, the heat in China was unbearable and Troy missed the demonstration, hooked up to a drip in his hotel room with severe dehydration. There was some suggestion that a few too many beers the previous night might have been a factor.

Back in Europe, there was more drama after the next round in Monza. This time we had nothing much to celebrate, although four top 10s at one of the fastest circuits, which was totally unsuited to our bike, was still encouraging. Oakley, one of our sponsors, was holding an event at the Hollywood nightclub in Milan that night, so we headed into the city after the race. By the time we finished dinner, it was probably knocking on midnight and there was nowhere to park, so I stuck the hire car right outside the nightclub entrance. Okay, it might have just been sticking out over some tramlines, but there was no way that trams would be running at that time of night, surely. Wrong. When we stumbled out three hours later, looking for a taxi, there was a big commotion around our car: police cars, flashing lights, a tow truck and two empty trams. Apparently, this was the main tram route into the centre of Milan and my parking had virtually brought the city's public transport network to a grinding halt. Passengers had to be bussed on to their destinations. The local coppers were pissed off and for a while it looked like I wouldn't need a taxi anywhere, because they would be giving me a lift to the nearest police station. Luckily Ruben Xaus, who speaks fluent Italian, was with us and explained to the policemen who I was. 'Ah, Foggy,' one of the coppers said, 'I am huge fan. Next time you park here all day and all night, per favore.' Okay, it didn't quite go like that, but I did escape with just a slapped wrist.

The results continued to go our way, Troy claiming our first pole position at the next round in Oschersleben. This was a circuit in the middle of nowhere, over the old border into former East Germany and not a place I was particularly bothered about visiting. Anyhow, I had made it clear at the start of the project that I didn't want to go to every round – I just wasn't ready for that commitment again. I wanted more time with my daughters Danielle and Claudia. My excuse for this round was that I was having an operation on my knee, which I'd actually had the previous week, and I felt terrible when Troy wished me a speedy recovery in his TV interview after winning Superpole with a typically effortless lap.

It turned out to be the only highlight of the rest of the season, until another pole position from Troy at the final round of Magny-Cours in France. There had been so much development work put into the engine, but still the same old problems with reliability remained. I was now convinced that the design of the engine was fundamentally flawed and I couldn't see any light at the end of the tunnel. Was it in Petronas' best interest to carry on with an uncompetitive bike? Could the road bike project not continue while the team painted up a competitive bike like a Fireblade or a Ducati in Petronas colours for the next two seasons? Unless the rules changed we were always going to be underpowered and never able to win in dry conditions. We couldn't increase the 900cc capacity without starting the homologation process all over again – and that just wasn't an option. I was trying to save their money and their reputation, but my suggestion didn't go down too well. Once they started something, they followed it through; anything else would have been seen as a loss of face. Sadly, it was also a period of change at Petronas. Madame Yati, who had been in charge of Project Misty, fell suddenly ill and passed away in November 2004. She was an impressive lady; a firm but fair businesswoman who also had a good sense of humour. Other key people within Petronas had moved on to different projects. And perhaps even Wongy had taken a bit of a backseat. It was clear the next couple of years were going to be even more of a struggle.

10

SPACE COWBOYS

The first task for 2005 was to find two new riders. Not surprisingly, both Chris and Troy wanted to be back on a competitive bike. Those three years must have been frustrating for Troy – he was a world-class rider, in a world-class team, but without a world-class bike. So I didn't bear him any grudges until some quotes appeared in the press about me, criticising my commitment and saying I had too many holidays. Looking back, he probably had a point. But there are always two sides to the story and he probably wasn't aware of the struggles I'd faced since retiring. He also said I wasn't much of a talker or communicator. It's true, I'm not. I never saw it as my job to advise the riders. If they were competing at world championship level, they didn't need to be told how to ride a bike. And it was difficult to try to motivate them when I was losing motivation myself. They would have seen right through that. I saw my role as trying to make sure that everything was right for the rider, so they could go out and do their best on any given day. And I did always fight their corner, although Troy might not have seen that. So I was angry he hadn't said this to my face and chose to go to the newspapers instead.

Petronas still expected a big-name rider and, perhaps surprisingly, we weren't short of options. People saw potential in the bike and the project. Word came back to us that the French rider, Regis Laconi, was willing to talk and we flew him over to England to have a look at our workshop and meet the team. He'd been runner-up the previous season and it amazed me that someone in his position was even willing to consider us.

We also made contact with Garry McCoy's management. This was a guy who had won five GPs, including two in 500s, and the 'Slide King' was a crowd-pleaser. He had been sixth in the World Superbike Championship the previous season with one of the satellite Ducati teams, including a win and two other podiums. But he was coming towards the end of his career and perhaps fancied a bit of a payday.

I was still keen on having at least one British rider and Shakey Byrne was top of that wanted list. He'd had a lean season in MotoGP with Aprilia but was keen to stay in that series, so I knew we would have to make him a good offer. The final rider in the equation was Steve Martin, a quiet but determined Aussie and probably one of the most underrated riders around at the time. He had stopped me in the paddock at one round and told me he'd be keen to be considered, but I didn't want to string him along and said there and then that there wasn't much chance. But we weren't going to be able to afford two big names, so the more I thought about it, the more he made sense.

Pick two from four – it all came down to the negotiations. The two guys we felt were most committed, and affordable, were McCoy and

Martin and I was able to replace riders who finished ninth and eleventh with the riders who finished sixth and seventh. The other new addition to the team was Jack Valentine, who replaced Steve Thompson as team manager. Thommo wanted to focus on the technical stuff again – and the new girlfriend that he'd met in Malaysia. Years later, I nearly choked on my brew when I saw them auditioning for *X Factor*. Simon Cowell was his usual charming self in telling them where to go.

Jack is a big, jolly no-nonsense Yorkshireman who ran his own team, ValMoto, for many years on the road racing circuit and in the British championships. He was the steady, experienced hand that we needed. There was just one problem. We couldn't get anything done at our board meetings with Jack around. Whenever it was his turn to report on team developments, his broad Yorkshire accent set us all off. There were two words in particular. Exhaust came out as 'eggs horst' and Qatar was 'kat tar'. Poor Jack just soldiered on through all the giggling until Michaela interrupted him at one meeting: 'Sorry, Jack, I'm going to have to stop you and explain why we're all laughing. Instead of saying Qatar, can you just say "that place in the desert!"'

With an all-Aussie line-up, I really had to show my face at Phillip Island, the circuit where it all ended for me. Instead of flying straight there me, Michaela and the girls stopped off in Far North Queensland and were joined by Neil for a few days. This was a place where you couldn't walk on the beach because of the crocodiles and couldn't swim in the sea because of box jellyfish. Great place for a holiday! The main attraction was obviously the Great Barrier Reef and we booked a day trip that included basic scuba-diving training. Claudia was too young but Danielle, who was only

10, was allowed to do it and that surprised me. Apparently, the sandbank we were stopping at was the nearest thing you could find to swimming pool conditions, so it was considered fine for kids. Danielle wasn't the one we should have been worried about, though. Bear in mind that Neil is the only person in the world ever to have been attacked by a dolphin. He was on holiday in Mexico and, when it was his turn to have his picture taken kissing the dolphin, it whacked him out of the pool with its tail. Michaela said it had probably never encountered a primate in its pool before.

Out at the sandbank and coral reef, we all put on our breathing apparatus and waded out into the deeper water. I could tell Neil was a bit nervous. Two minutes later, he was at the surface flailing his arms around, trying to attract the attention of the instructor. He had been concentrating so hard on inhaling regularly that he had forgotten to fully exhale, so his lungs were over-inflated. The instructor gave him another chance, as long as he stayed close to him.

The water wasn't actually that clear because there had been a storm the previous day, so there weren't many fish to see. But that didn't matter because, when I looked down, I could see Neil strolling hand-in-hand with the instructor on the seabed. I caught Michaela's attention and we both had to get out of the water because we used up too much oxygen crying into our masks.

Going back to Phillip Island, five years after my crash, was quite an emotional experience for me and I did some interviews for the local press at the spot where I crashed. It also brought back fond memories of clinching my first World Superbike title in 1994, too. The preparation for that final round had not been ideal, to say the least. Scott Russell had slashed my championship lead down to just five points at Donington, when the wet tyre I used for the first race had no grip as the rain came down. It was wet again for the second race and, although I was on a much better soft wet rear, I knew I couldn't push too hard and throw away all my points advantage. So I sat in fifth, expecting Ducati riders Troy Corser and Mauro Lucchiari to let me through towards the end under team orders. But their signal never came, and my team boss Virginio Ferrari said that it was not how he wanted to win the title. But he wasn't riding, I was. At the time I was furious and shouted my mouth off in the newspapers. Some people aren't keen on team orders, but it's a no-brainer to me. When a team is paying you a lot of money, and you can help your team-mate win a world title, then of course you should accept team orders. It benefits everyone. I'm not sure I would have been that keen to follow team orders when I was racing, though. I would probably have been like Lorenzo at the final MotoGP in 2017, when he ignored a coded instruction to switch to 'Mapping 8' – roughly translated as 'Let Dovi pass, for f**k's sake!'

It was good to be in Australia and far away from that team-orders cock-up, and at a circuit that suited my style of carrying a lot of corner speed, but I was tense at the start of the first race and almost crashed at Siberia, which would have effectively handed the title to Russell. I pulled myself together, passed Russell early on and put in fast lap after fast lap to win the race and extend my lead to eight points. All I had to do was follow him round in race two and the title was mine. I did just that until, with three laps remaining, he waved me through, almost like he was throwing in the towel. It was bizarre that he pulled into the pits next time round, because he would have won the championship if anything had happened to my bike. It was my fourth world title, after my two Formula One TT titles and World Endurance Championship, but it was the first one that got any kind of recognition in the British press.

So Phillip Island was a place of mixed emotions for me, and emotions were running high on the grid for the first race of 2005. Steve started the season with a bang when he was just 0.06 s off pole position behind Yukio Kagayama on the Suzuki, one of the best superbikes I have ever seen. More importantly, he beat Troy, who was also riding for Suzuki, by 0.1 s. Troy came up to me to shake my hand on the grid, but his comments in the press were still raw and I had nothing to say to him.

There was another brief stop-off in Malaysia on the way home for another street demonstration, this time in Kuala Lumpur and again with the F1 team. Jacques Villeneuve had joined Massa and was a bit of a strange character. You normally find that F1 drivers only want to talk about bikes. I think they appreciate that it's more difficult to ride on two wheels than drive on four, and so they have a real respect for bike racers. But I felt Villeneuve only wanted to talk about himself. If I mentioned that I had a new jet-ski, he had four which were better. If I mentioned Michaela, he brought up Danni Minogue. Okay, I didn't mind that so much, especially some of the stories. Better not say any more!

Back in Europe, our season basically went downhill all the way. Out of 24 races throughout the season, our riders either crashed, retired or could not start 23 times. If anything, the reliability of the engine was even worse and, while there had been a few positives to take from 2004 and some hope that we were going in the right direction, there was precious little to smile about. On the track at least.

Just about the only thing that kept me sane was having my mates around me for most of the European rounds, including Assen. I had reasonably high hopes there, because it was another of the circuits that should have suited our bike better than other tracks. Instead, our best result of the weekend was twelfth from Garry, so we were ready to drown our sorrows on the Sunday night.

A lot of Brits always head over to Assen. Someone estimated that 40,000 travelled there in 1999 to watch what turned out to be my final double win there. But when we wandered around the nearby city of Groningen after the races, I started to wonder whether I had been the main attraction after all. We turned down one side street to find it packed with hundreds of middle-aged British men, tongues on the pavement, leering at the prossies in the windows. Down the next street was one of the local coffee shops, also packed with Brits – including my mate Mark. When we sat down in the main square for a beer, he unwrapped some greaseproof paper and started handing out the space cakes he'd bought.

'Here, get this down yer neck, fella,' he laughed. 'This'll cheer you up!'

'Go on then, suppose it can't hurt,' I said, picking the smallest piece. Ten minutes later, nothing had happened. 'Have you got any left? That one was shit,' I asked Mark. This time I went for a bigger piece. Ten minutes later, not a thing. 'Give us some more. I'm actually hungry,' I said, grabbing the last crumbs.

Another 10 minutes and my new trainers were the funniest thing I'd ever seen in my life. I was sitting in the main square of Groningen, bike fans everywhere, and pissing myself laughing at a pair of shoes.

'What's the matter with you?' Michaela asked.

'It's me trainers,' I just about managed to say.

'What about them?' she said, looking under the table.

'They're just so funny,' I wheezed, holding on to my chair like grim death. Everyone ignored me and carried on with their banter. But I could hear what people were saying three tables away.

'Mmmmmmfffff!' Shit, that wasn't what I was trying to say. I was trying to tell someone, anyone, that I needed a pee and that I couldn't move. I tried again: 'Mmmmmmfffff!'

'Carl, stop it, you're being an idiot,' Michaela said. For about 30 minutes, I tried to form some sounds that would make it clear that I needed to piss, but all I could do was grunt like I had a gag in my mouth. Finally, Mark said, 'Right, I'm off to the bog', so I started bouncing up and down, nodding my head. 'Mmmmmff! Mmmmmff!'

'Ah, you need a piss. Come on then,' he said and virtually had to carry me into the pub, and back out. By then, everyone else who'd had some cake was starting to get giddy and someone suggested it might be an idea for us not to be out in public any longer.

'Mmmmmff! Mmmmmff!' I bounced up and down again. That was exactly what I wanted and someone put me in a taxi with one of Michaela's friends, who was also starting to struggle. When the driver asked us in a Dutch accent where we were going, we just pissed ourselves laughing again. It took us 10 minutes to tell him the name of the hotel and the taxi driver was losing his rag. 'Get a grip,' I told myself and spent the whole journey trying to avoid eye contact with either of them. Back at the hotel, someone was waiting at reception to lead me to my room. By now the effect was wearing off a bit, but the world was spinning. I made it to the lift, just as the doors opened on a middle-aged couple heading out for a romantic evening together. Right on cue, I threw up all over them. That night probably wasn't the most responsible thing I have ever done.

The decision on riders for 2006 was nowhere near as complicated. Garry's best finish all season was eleventh and there really was no point in paying a big name to ride such an uncompetitive bike. Steve's best result on the track was fifth in the first race at Imola. The start of the second race was delayed there when the heavens opened while the riders were on the grid. The mechanics quickly pushed the bikes back into the pits and the riders were sheltered by their brolly girls. All except Steve – and it was one of the few times I saw him really pissed off. Neil was responsible for choosing the brolly girls, but some of the mechanics had been chatting up a local girl who was working at one of the merchandise stalls and persuaded Neil to let her hold Steve's brolly for the second race. The only problem was that Neil was so busy letching after the umbrella girl on the grid that he gormlessly wandered back to the pits under the brolly with her – and Steve returned to the garage looking like a drowned rat. He could have been racing again 20 minutes later and his leathers were soaking, but luckily the second race was cancelled. Can you imagine if that had happened to me when I was racing?

That was the least of Steve's problems, but he was the ultimate professional. He knew the limitations of the bike and, although he was obviously frustrated, he got on with the job to the best of his ability without whinging or moaning. I say that Imola was Steve's best result on the track. In fact, his best result was probably at the final round of Magny-Cours, when he was involved in a nasty four-bike pile-up at the first corner. One of the

Above: With my dad in 1983 at my first ever race at Aintree just after my eighteenth birthday. Nice New Romantic hairstyle…

Below: On the start line of a schoolboy motocross race in 1982. I'm number 3 (third from the left) and probably not about to win.

Above: Leading Nick Jefferies (7) and Steve Hislop (11) over the leap at Cronk-y-Voddy during the final practice for the 1991 TT.

Left: Knackered after an epic battle with Dave Leach and Steve Hislop to win my first TT in 1989.

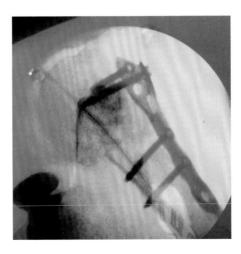

Above: Hard as nails. Here's the metalwork in my shoulder after my crash at Phillip Island. It's still in there.

Left: Having a wheelie good time on a CCM supermoto in 2001.

Below: On my way to my fourth World Superbike title in 1999.

Above: Mucking about at my local MX track.

Below: Sitting pretty in front of the Petronas Twin Towers in Kuala Lumpur to launch the FP1 road bike.

Left: At the launch of La Vache restaurant with Lawrence Dallaglio and James Blunt. Don't remember too much after that shot!

Below: Jaws ache. Grappling with a huge tope, a member of the shark family, to win a fishing cup in memory of my mate Mark Winstanley.

Left: Feeling a right tit. Mark cops a feel as we get ready to go and watch *The Rocky Horror Picture Show.*

Below: Three unwise monkeys. Mark, me and my mate, Kev Moore, at a local motocross event. I really miss those days.

Above left: Nice arse. I'll have the ostrich's anus, please.
Above right: Michaela comes running onto the *I'm a Celebrity* bridge at one of the happiest moments of my life.

Above left: 'King of the Jungle'; with his queen, Michaela, and two princesses, Claudia and Danielle.

Above right: Practising my poker face during a competition for partypoker, which I won. Not sure how…

Left: My jungle mate, Jimmy Bullard, dicking around as usual during filming for an episode of *Play to the Whistle*.

Flat out. Having fun with some skids and slides at Buxton Speedway.

Above: Shady character! Prospective son-in-law Jake Quickenden makes a good brolly girl.

Left: Scrubbed up. With Michaela at an awards ceremony.

Left: Cool dad. A nice summer's day in Mellor with Claudia and Danielle.

bikes smacked him in the stomach and he was given the all-clear by doctors at first. But when he started pissing blood, they sent him for a scan and found a massive tumour in one of his kidneys. The only option was to remove the whole kidney and tests later found that it had been malignant. It's fair to say that the crash saved his life, as it's unlikely it would have been discovered in time otherwise. So the season wasn't all bad.

FOGGY PHENOMENA
10 films

Rocky

One Flew Over the Cuckoo's Nest

The Simpsons Movie

The Lion King

Jaws

The Hangover

George Formby's No Limit

Get Him to the Greek

Pirates of the Caribbean

King Kong

11

REGRETS, I'VE HAD A FEW

It was soon clear that Petronas would not continue their sponsorship beyond 2006. Who could blame them? The whole thing had been a bit of a PR disaster for them – and an expensive one. Sure, they were seen to have pushed the boundaries of engineering, something that was important for their image. But unfortunately, those boundaries had been too challenging and there was precious little to shout about. The road bike project had similar problems, too. By 2005, only a handful had been sold to the public in Malaysia and I genuinely didn't know what happened to the rest of the 150 bikes, until a Malaysian company called Momoto contacted me years later. They bought the intellectual property off Petronas and Momoto was keen to have me involved again, but then there was a legal battle with Petronas about some technicality and their interest fizzled out.

It was a no-brainer to keep Steve Martin on for another season, as he'd been my favourite of all our riders so far. But there was no point going for another big name to be his team-mate. We could have had Valentino Rossi on the bike and it wouldn't have made any difference. So I was very keen to give a young British rider an opportunity and throw him in at the deep end. Jack had run a young kid called Craig Jones on a Triumph in the British Supersport Championship for a couple of years and Craig had also caught my attention with a couple of impressive rides. I sounded out James Whitham and former Sky Sports commentator Keith Huewen, who spent more time in the British paddock than me and knew all the emerging talents. Both agreed that Craig was as good as any of the new crop such as Cal Crutchlow, Leon Camier, Tom Sykes and Jonathan Rea.

As usual there were a few people in the team who didn't think it was such a good idea, but this time I put my foot down. I could see so much of myself in Craig. I'd learnt the hard way in World Superbikes in 1991 on a slow bike. The experience can really set you up for the future. The challenge for me was to try and calm Craig down. He crashed during practice at the first round in Qatar and, while he was having a piece of gravel plucked out of his knee in the medical centre, he was desperate to get back out there before the end of the session. I told him: 'Look, take it easy. You have all season. Stay on the bike, get to know it, and aim to be beating your team-mate by the end of the season. That's all I'm asking.' Then he crashed after a couple of laps of the first race. 'Look, just finish the next race, for f**k's sake,' I said. He came through start-finish in race two like a man possessed, set his fastest lap of the whole weekend on lap 3 . . . and then crashed again. I think Craig was expecting a right bollocking but that wouldn't have achieved anything, although I was a bit annoyed. 'Right, I've tried telling you,' I said. 'Now I'm not going to say anything else. The bike's not the best thing out there. It's up to you how you want to ride it.' On the way out of the garage, I couldn't help smiling to myself. I saw so much of myself in Craig's attitude. By the end of the year he was as fast as Steve, which was just about the only positive thing we could take from another dismal season. We scored 18 points in total, 210 less than any other manufacturer.

If I was going to continue as a team owner, we had to run a competitive bike that would attract good sponsorship and the best riders. Ducati was the obvious first option, but first we had to find a major sponsor and that was never going to be easy at the level of funding we'd received from Petronas. Some teams could survive on a budget of £100,000. We needed that to pay the rates. But it did look promising when, out of the blue, Neil received an e-mail from the Italian representative of an Israeli billionaire called Lev Leviev, known as the 'King of Diamonds'. He requested to meet us in Milan because Leviev had surplus funds that he wanted to invest in various projects so that he could reduce his tax bill.

Me, Neil and Murray arranged to meet him in a café off the main square and sat there for half an hour before we received a mysterious call. Change of plan. They wanted to meet on the other side of the square. So off we trotted and knocked on the door of a restaurant, which was clearly closed. A shady-looking bloke opened the door, checked if anyone was watching, then let us in and told us to wait in a curtained-off back room. Something smelled a bit fishy, and it wasn't the spaghetti marinara. Then another couple of dodgy characters entered the room, sat down and placed a briefcase between us on the table. One of them launched into a long-winded account of how the transaction would take place, which included about seven transfers of millions of dollars all around Europe, the Cayman Islands, Monaco and eventually into a Swiss bank account. Yeah, right. I didn't have a clue what he was on about, but I knew something didn't add up. They could see we were not interested and one of them leaned over, looking very serious.

'If you do not believe we have the money, look at this,' he said, opening the briefcase. I hadn't seen that much cash since Michaela's last shopping spree. There must have been a couple of million Euros – or Monopoly money, perhaps. Their henchmen were now blocking the door to make sure no-one could see in, get in – or get out. I was starting to feel a bit twitchy, so we quickly made our excuses, promised them we would think about it and legged it into the nearest bar. No surprises then, that when we did a bit of digging, Leviev knew nothing about this and put out a press statement warning everyone to beware of people pretending to represent him.

The rider we were building our hopes of attracting sponsorship around was my old team-mate, rival and friend, Neil Hodgson – though things hadn't been too friendly between us for a while. When Neil moved to MotoGP in 2004 after his World Superbike title, he pissed me off by saying I had been too scared to race against Mick Doohan. Really?

I regret not having the chance to go to GPs. People say you shouldn't have regrets, but that's bollocks. I regret having that extra-hot curry last night. I regret running out of fuel on the last lap of the British Grand Prix in 1993. Who wouldn't regret that? Maybe I wasn't given that Marlboro Yamaha ride by Kenny Roberts in 1996 because of the way I spoke to people or handled myself back then. I regret that, too. Knowing what I know now, I would certainly have done things differently. But there is no question

I would have won races on the Marlboro Yamaha, which would have suited my style. Would I have beaten Doohan and become world champion? I can't answer that. Nobody can. But when Doohan finished, and before Rossi came along, I would have only had to beat people who raced like me – the likes of Biaggi, Capirossi, Cadalora and Checa. Were these guys faster than me? Were they more determined? Max Biaggi was possibly as determined, but certainly not more. I would have challenged for the world title in that era, no question whatsoever. When Cal Crutchlow became the first Brit to win a premier class GP since Barry Sheene in 1981, they should have been saying 'the first Brit to win a premier class GP since Carl Fogarty in the mid-to-late 90s'. I think most so-called experts at the time knew I would have challenged for wins and possibly the world title but didn't want to admit it because they were so far up the arses of Doohan, Rainey and Schwantz. And now it annoys them that I have achieved fame and fortune without ever winning a GP. There is a lot of jealousy in this sport.

Phew. I'm glad I got that off my chest.

Anyhow, I couldn't let Neil Hodgson's comments go unanswered and had a go back at him in the press, calling him boring and saying that he was handed his world title because there was nobody to beat. I regret saying that, too. Neil rode really well that year and would probably have beaten the likes of Colin Edwards. But you can only beat the people you are racing against.

His year in MotoGP did not work out and he went to the American Superbike Championship for a couple of years. Although he was on good money, he felt he had unfinished business in World Superbikes. Ducati told me that Bayliss saw him as too much of a threat and were therefore not interested. So we tried to put together a package around him and he flew out to Magny-Cours for FPR's final race to meet the team and get a feel for how we did things.

It soon became clear that we wouldn't have a sponsor for 2007, which left Neil high and dry. And Ducati were now saying that they would not be able to provide much support for 2007, because the championship was struggling to compete with MotoGP, which was now their number one focus. So we needed a change of direction and, early in 2007, we announced our intention to run the MV Augusta F4 R 312 as their factory team. I had known the MV president Claudio Castiglioni since my early days with Ducati, which was then owned by his Cagiva group, and we had always got on well. MV had been planning a return to racing for a while and saw our team as the perfect match for their image and ambitions. But we still needed a sponsor and, with our mechanics and staff all on a retainer, money and time – and patience – were running out.

We planned a meeting with Claudio at the Monza round in May and I was due to fly out on the Saturday morning, straight after finishing a coast-to-coast charity enduro ride with Kev for an air ambulance charity. We finished in Scarborough late on the Friday night and I decided to stay the night there in a police barracks, so we had virtually no sleep. I was wrecked in the morning, from lack of sleep and the riding, and jumping on a plane to Italy was the last thing I wanted to do. Murray and Neil were already out there and I called Murray to tell him I wouldn't be coming. I'd already spoken to Claudio and he was fine with it. But Murray went off on one, telling me that I needed to show more commitment. That really pissed me off. I'd just been busting my balls for charity for two days.

It wasn't as though I hadn't been trying to find a sponsor. Just a few weeks earlier me, my manager Neil and Michaela had been in Dubai. I was the guest of honour at the Dubai Manx Society charity banquet, but in the backs of our minds we wanted to make some wealthy connections. The owner of the Dubai Autodrome was on that list, but not for long. After taking me on a 'fast' lap in his Ferrari, he gave me a go in the driver's seat but was begging for me to stop after a few corners. Well, he did tell me to go as fast as I wanted. At the banquet we were introduced to the winner of the local championship, who just happened to be a distant relative of Osama bin Laden. We even thought of a plan for him to support the team financially in return for a ride in the World Supersport Championship.

Then I took part in the Isle of Man TT centenary celebrations, where I rode the MV in the Parade of Champions to try and put us under the noses of potential sponsors. All the big names were there on the bikes that made them famous. I was riding an MV Augusta, but it just felt wrong. And I'm sure Ducati were not best pleased to hear me bigging up MV as the Ferrari of the two-wheel world at every opportunity. We flew out to Misano for really promising meetings with Hannspree and Philip Morris Tobacco. We had a sponsorship agent with a good track record in F1 deals on a costly retainer. He lined up a deal with a porn company, Private, but that fell through the cracks. (What a blow. It was really hard-on us!) By the time we went to Brands in August for one last throw of the dice, it was pretty obvious we were not going to get this thing off the ground. Neil was getting twitchy, too. He couldn't afford another season on the sidelines and, not surprisingly, he accepted a new ride in the American Superbike Championship.

We had tried everything in our powers, but we were now out of money and there was no other option but to shut it all down and sell up – the premises, trucks, equipment, memorabilia, every last nut and bolt. It was a sad end to a part of my career that, if things had been different, I could and should have looked back on with pride. I did enjoy bits of it, but mostly it was a tough personal struggle. And at the end of it all, I felt that racing had rejected me.

Then came the real hammer blow. Craig Jones, the one rider who I felt I'd been able to help, was killed at Brands Hatch in August of 2008. He was dicing for the lead of the World Supersport round with Jonathan Rea when he crashed coming onto the start-finish and was hit by the foot-peg of Australian rider Andrew Pitt's bike. I was so upset and angry. I felt he was over-riding a bike that did not match his talent. This was a lad, and a great lad at that, who was destined to be a world champion, in my opinion. His funeral, especially when the coffin arrived draped in an English flag with his number 18, was too much to take. I felt I needed to get as far away from racing as possible again.

12

MARKED MAN

The positive thing about the team coming to an end was that I could spend more time with the lads, trail-riding, motocrossing or mucking about on the water with jet-skis or water-skis. I felt I could be myself around this bunch of scoundrels – having a laugh, a few beers and a curry. But you could never ever relax, especially around Mark, who I was spending more and more time with and had become one of my best mates. If you dropped your guard for a split second, he would make you pay.

For example, if you left your backpack unattended during a break on a trail-ride, he would stick a rock in it and you'd be carrying it around all afternoon. If you left your gloves on the table of a café while you went to the bog, they would be filled with ketchup when you came back. I have seen him fill someone's motocross boots with duck shit or stick a dead frog in their water-skiing boots. One of his favourite tricks was to smear black boot polish on the inside of the neck of a dry suit so that when the owner squeezed into it, their hair and face would be covered in the stuff. He would get up at 5 am to prepare that one.

At one motocross race, all the vans were parked on either side of the dirt track running through the field. The next race was announced and everyone got up to go and watch. 'Woah, don't be going anywhere yet, lad,' Mark said. He then disappeared into the van, brought out a carton of 24 eggs and wandered casually down both rows of vans, dropping eggs into the riders' boots that had been left out to air. When the race ended, everyone made their way back to their vans and started to get ready for their next race. 'Watch this,' said Mark, sitting back with a grin like the Cheshire cat. It went just as he planned. All along the line people were pulling on their boots and shouting: 'What the f**k?' But they blamed the bloke parked next to them, and not us, because we were right at the far end, rolling around Mark's van in hysterics. A couple of the guys were close to coming to blows.

It was tough to get revenge on Mark, though. We were once in a café in Hawes in the Lake District for lunch and Mark was the only one of us to order pudding, apple pie and whipped cream. 'Just going to the bog,' he said, packing everything into his bag to take with him to the toilet, realising we were looking for an opportunity to get him back. 'You have to get up bloody early to catch a weasel and piss in its ear,' he laughed. That was one of his favourite sayings. Mark reached the door on the far side of the café when he panicked and looked around to see the waitress putting his apple pie and cream down on the table. This was our big chance. I had the bottle of ketchup in my hand ready to squirt into the centre of the cream and Kev had Mark's spoon in his hand.

'Noooooooooooo ...' he screamed. He launched himself across the room, scattering tables, chairs, women and children left, right and centre and belly-dived onto the table to rescue his apple pie. Too late. Kev had stuffed as much as was physically possible into his mouth already. So Mark slammed Kev's face into what was left on the plate. I was pleading with him to believe me that the sauce wasn't meant for him, otherwise I would be wearing it. The staff and other customers looked on in disbelief.

It might have been during the same ride-out, on a freezing, wet winter's day, that we had to cross what is normally a small, rocky stream. On this day it was like the River Nile. The last thing anyone wanted to do was fall, because they would be freezing for the rest of the ride. Mark went first and managed to stay upright by putting his feet down on the rocky bed all the way across, but I could tell he was knackered. He took his helmet and goggles off and leant on a gate to catch his breath. Kev was next up and we could all see he was struggling. He was more than halfway across when Mark appeared from the other side of the gate, staggering towards Kev and holding a disgusting dead sheep over his head. Just as he was about to launch it and try to knock Kev off, the legs separated from the rotting body and the stomach of the sheep exploded over Mark's head in a heap of maggots. Mark was standing there holding a leg in each hand and covered in stinking sheep flesh. I think Kev did actually fall over laughing and the rest of us on the other bank couldn't breathe for half an hour. When Kev did finally make it across, Mark stuffed a sackful of sheep shit inside his open-faced helmet.

We already know from the boat stories that some of Mark's genius mechanical projects don't always go to plan. But his attempt to build a Cobra replica kit car with a Rover V8 engine was a disaster from the word go. When he thought it was finished, he rang me and Kev and said: 'Get round here tonight, the beast is running.' Okay, it was running but had no seats or seat belts. It was a shell on wheels and he was expecting me to sit on a milk crate next to him. 'F**k that,' I said. 'Kev, you have a go.'

I saw them disappear round a couple of bends and then it all went quiet. 'Hold on, boy, warp factor nine, here we come,' he'd told Kev as he floored it. Both milk crates shot to the back. Unfortunately, Mark was still holding the steering wheel, because he'd forgotten to put the retaining nut on the splined shaft. The car flew into a hedge, with the back end poking out into the road. 'Now then, how f**king fast was that, boy,' he said to Kev. A couple of minutes later, who should arrive on the scene but the local village bobby.

'Now then, young Winstanley, what have we here?' the copper asked.

'I've just built this car and took my mate Kev out for a spin in this field when it shot backward through this hedge. As you can plainly see, we were most definitely not driving a car without an MOT on a public high-way, officer,' said Mark. The copper laughed, shook his head and told us to get it back home on a trailer.

When he finally finished the Cobra, he was gutted that it was so slow. So he forked out £12,000 on a new 600 bhp V8 engine from the USA. He took it out on his own one summer evening and a few lads in a Subaru pulled up behind him, revving away. Red rag to a bull . . . Mark floored it again and it spat him out, sending him flying down the road on his arse and straight into another hedge. He hadn't thought to set the tracking and suspension to cope with the power of the engine. The thing was a death trap, but he walked away with just a bit of nasty gravel rash.

Unfortunately, it wasn't only Mark who paid the price for his blatant disregard for human safety. He once bought a double parasail to pull behind his truck and took it down to Pilling Sands near Heysham to try it out on the beach. It went surprisingly well and a few of his mates got up in the air in tandem and back down without incident. Then the middle-aged parents of one of the lads asked to have a go. Again, everything was going fine and the couple were high up in the air until, for some reason known only to himself, Mark decided to take his boots off. But as he was messing about with his boots, he slowed down without realising. The others were waving frantically and trying to catch his attention because the couple lost height really quickly and thudded down into the sand – two broken legs for the man and one for the woman. The worst part was that he dragged them down the beach for half a mile because he hadn't noticed they'd come down.

Another not-so-bright idea was to try and recreate a barefoot water-skiing stunt from the James Bond movie *Licence to Kill* – Mark Winstanley-style. In the film, James Bond was being attacked by some villains on the seabed and, to escape from them, he harpooned a sea-plane. It dragged him to the surface and he barefooted behind the plane to safety. Instead of the experienced stuntman used in the film, Mark decided to try out his idea using his young apprentice as a volunteer/guinea pig. The lad swam down to the bottom of the lake with the handle and Mark nailed the boat. But he started to worry when the lad failed to appear for a while. Everyone was peering anxiously over the side when suddenly out popped the apprentice like a jumping salmon, still holding manfully on to the ski handle, cheeks bulging with water and choking on bits of weed. He didn't volunteer for a repeat run.

So this man might have been a danger to himself and anyone around him, but Mark was a lovable rogue with a heart of gold who lived life to the full. He would do anything for a mate and, because he ran his own plastering company, had loads of free time to spend with me, especially when the race team had finished.

Then, in the summer of 2007, we were motocrossing at a sand track near Southport when he first complained of a pain in his stomach. And Mark was not one to complain, believe me. He went to be checked out by the doctors who told him that he had stomach cancer and probably only had between two and five years to live. It would have hit him like a tonne of bricks but, outwardly at least, he took it in his stride. He was more bothered about the futures of his wife and girls. It was the same attitude that another good mate, James Whitham, has shown with both his cancer scares. He just gets on with it, accepts whatever treatment is recommended and doesn't let it get in the way of life. I think I would probably have the same attitude, if it ever happened to me. If it was a member of my family, though, I'm not sure I would be able to cope in the same way.

Mark was really positive about a big and risky operation to remove a lot of his stomach and, for a while after that, he seemed to be pulling through. He even put some weight back on. Then, slowly and before our eyes, this 16-stone man-mountain was whittled away to around half that weight over the next year or so. It wasn't easy to watch, but he loved coming with me to bike shows and events or going out fishing on the boat.

This was a time when I didn't want to watch any racing. I still felt rejected because we hadn't found the money to continue the team. I wouldn't have known who won the world championships in 2007, 2008 or 2009. I'd slipped back into whinging and moaning about my own sport – and usually to Mark.

'Will you stop trying to forget who you are,' he told me, when he was very sick. 'Start celebrating your achievements. You should be proud, not bitter and angry. Life has been so good to you. You are the best rider ever in the sport that you love. But look at you now, you hate it. Get back involved in your sport. Embrace it. What do you have to moan about? Look at me, I'm dying, for f**k's sake.'

Mark passed away on 15 February 2010. His last wish was that he could build a big new house for his family in time – and he succeeded. That was the measure of the man, always putting other people first. He was a great friend to everyone, and me and Michaela visited him many times during his last few days in the hospice. His wife asked me to help carry the coffin at his funeral and I have never seen so many people turn out. It was impossible for me to keep it together, but we were determined to celebrate his life that night. Just before he passed, Mark told us that he wanted his best mates to get pissed and go for a curry at his favourite Indian, the Shajan. We did him proud.

There was such a big hole to fill when he was gone but his words have stayed with me every day. Whenever I feel negative about something, I think back to what he said and try to snap out of it.

And I did become more involved with the sport. I spent most of the 2011 season as a pundit for Eurosport, both in the London studio and also on-site at Silverstone for WSBK and some BSB rounds. I have never been interested in commentating. It's not something I would be particularly good at. Others are good at it. James and Jack Burnicle were very good together, but the best double-act was Julian Ryder and Keith Huewen, and it's a shame that Julian has retired. He is a complete anorak of motor-cycling stats and figures and a great commentator, although I wouldn't want to be stuck in a cramped commentary box with him on a hot day.

I much prefer the studio work to the live on-site stuff. It's more relaxing and I can think about what I'm going to say, before and after the race. At the circuits, we are stuck at the end of the pit-lane with distractions everywhere, equipment that sometimes doesn't work and numpties jumping up and down behind you pulling faces. I told Eurosport halfway through the season that I wasn't enjoying the on-site rounds, but they wanted me to do a few more. I told them I would see how I felt after the Donington round of BSB, but the decision was taken out of my hands.

We were about to go live at about 10 am when my co-presenter, Tony Carter, said: 'I can't hear Carl's mike.' So someone in the studio then said: 'Carl, can you say something please? Tony can't hear you.' I didn't know what to say, but I was looking at Tony and thought I might as well talk about him.

'I'm standing here in pit-lane at Donington looking at Tony Carter, a fat ginger f**ker who is hopeless at presenting this show.'

One of the bosses back in the studio must have nearly choked on his cornflakes and the message came back via one of the producers: 'Carl, please be careful with the language you use when we are off air.' That was the point – it was a rehearsal, not live on air. Tony laughed it off and I didn't think any more about it until Neil received an e-mail from Euro-sport saying that, due to my choice of words during equipment testing at Donington, my services were no longer required. They tried to make out that Tony had complained, but I know that wasn't true. I got on well with him and thought he did a good job. He was a bit of a fan, so I knew this was just an excuse for them to stop using me, which didn't worry me one bit. After a couple of years, they approached me again and I still do the occasional appearance, so it couldn't have been that big a deal.

Anyway, now I'm back in love with the sport of bike racing. It made me a success, but also changed me as a person when I was racing, and I regret that. Mark helped me find the real, fun-loving, happy-go-lucky Carl Fogarty again. And his words never had more impact than when a certain reality TV show contacted me a couple of years later.

FOGGY PHENOMENA
10 places where I have eaten

Cami de Balafia, Ibiza

Chicken, steak or rabbit and chips.

La Vache, Verbier

Check out the Foggy pizza.

Otelo, Tenerife

Tenerife's version of KFC, but ten times better.

La Tor, La Villa, Italy

Ham, cheese, spicy salami and red onion pizza.

Villa Tiberio, Marbella

See if you can spot me on the wall.

China Tang, London

Pork and prawn dim sum.

The Cliff, Barbados

Most beautiful setting in the world.

Spread Eagle, Blackburn

Steak and ale pie, chips and peas. My local.

Shajan, Mellor, Blackburn

Chicken banjara, pilau rice, garlic naan.

Scarlet, Barbados

Baxter's Road fried chicken.

13

JUNGLE FEVER

'No way, you're not doing it, forget it.' It's fair to say Michaela was pretty adamant that she was not keen on the idea of me going on *I'm a Celebrity . . . Get Me Out of Here!* I was first approached by ITV shortly after my retirement, and she was actually quite up for it at that time. But, with everything that was going on around the team and the space I was in personally, it was not the best timing and I turned it down. Then my manager, Neil, got another call early in 2013. Did I want to go down to London for an informal chat with the bosses of the show?

I didn't see any harm in going to meet them. This was the one reality show that I actually watched and enjoyed. I had often wondered, especially after that first approach, how I would cope in there. I quite fancied the challenge – and that's the right reason for doing it. Others might see it as a chance to reinvent themselves, or to put themselves in the shop window for careers in TV, but I didn't need or want to do either of those things. I knew that nothing in the jungle itself would scare me – the things I would struggle with were lack of food, boredom and the other celebrities. This is why Michaela saw it differently. She knows what I'm like when I'm hungry, bored or irritated by someone. 'You'll hate it,' she said. 'You'll be kicking off all the time. It will make you look bad.' I guess Michaela was just expressing reasonable concerns for her husband's reputation, especially when she knew exactly what I was like when I was racing.

So off I trotted down to London, not really knowing what to expect. The team there were very welcoming and we asked each other lots of questions about the show, including: 'What would scare you the most?'

'Being caught on camera having a wank behind a tree,' I joked.

One of the producers spat her coffee all over the table and, luckily, the others laughed too. I could see them thinking: 'This guy's not wired right. We want him on the show.'

I told them about Michaela's worries, so they agreed to travel up to Blackburn to try and put her mind at ease. That helped a bit, but not enough. The timing wasn't great, either. Michaela was due to have an operation on her shoulder around that time, and my mum was really ill with a rare form of dementia. Nobody expected her to last much longer, and I was worried about something happening to her while I was in the jungle. It made sense to tell ITV that I was still interested, but we would have to wait until the following year. I fully expected that to be the end of it all, but they came back straightaway in March 2014. We named a take-it-or-leave it fee and, when they accepted this, I was well and truly on the spot. It was decision time.

Michaela was still dead against it, but the girls were both keen, Neil thought it would be good for me and a few of my friends were very encouraging. A couple of people thought it was beneath me, but they weren't fans of the show. This was the biggest thing on UK television – how could it be beneath me? The first person I had to fully convince, though, was myself. I'd watched the previous season and still had a few niggling worries. What if I didn't make it to the first vote-off without walking out? What if I didn't come across well? Would my anxiety issues take over? And then I stopped tying myself in knots when Mark's words came back to me. 'Start celebrating who you are. Get out there. Embrace it.'

'F**k it. I don't care what anyone else thinks, it's my decision. Let's do this,' I thought.

It was a few weeks before I plucked up the courage to tell Michaela, though. She wanted nothing to do with it, and that summer was a tense period in the Foggy household. 'I'm going to show you I can do this,' I thought. Once all the contracts were signed and sealed, I had to go back down to London for the cloak-and-dagger publicity shots. Then I went for a very weird interview at the home of the show's resident psychologist, who wasn't afraid to get down to the nitty gritty.

'How's your sex life, Carl?'

'Great, thanks. How's yours?'

'Are you afraid of snakes?'

'Is that question related?'

'Have you ever suffered from depression?'

'Well, I'm not too happy right now . . .'

I could tell she was getting a bit frustrated that I wasn't taking her seriously, and after a while I just told her the answers she wanted to hear so that I could get out of there. I didn't mention anything about my problems with anxiety or depression.

With just a week to go before I left for Australia, I could tell that Michaela was starting to come round. Some of the lads organised a table at a Blackburn Rovers game, and I really wasn't all that fussed about going. We set off ridiculously early in Chris Monk's car, because he said he needed to put some air in a tyre. His tyres looked okay to me. Then we hung around for ages after the game and, when we finally made it back home, Chris told me to use the side entrance. Eh? I opened the door and *I'm a Celebrity* music blared out, party poppers went off everywhere, inflatable crocs were hanging from the ceiling and everyone was wearing Ant and Dec masks. The surprise party was Michaela's way of saying: 'I'm right behind you now.'

Leaving home a few days later was quite emotional. I was shitting myself at that point. I knew that I wouldn't be seeing Michaela again until I crossed that famous bridge – if I hadn't walked out before then. It would be the longest time we'd ever been without contact since we'd been together. It would be weird not speaking to each other every day. Security was waiting at Brisbane Airport to whisk me past the reporters and into a limo where my personal minder, a Kiwi lady, said I could make one last call before my mobile was taken off me. So there were more tears from Michaela before we finally said goodbye.

The minder's job was to follow my every move for about seven days. I was one of the first to arrive and I was glad of that. I'm usually terrible with jet-lag and I wanted to be on Australian time zone when the show started. At the hotel, I went straight to sleep and woke up late afternoon. There was no one about, so I wandered down to the pool and then onto the beach for a stroll. She was waiting for me when I got back to the hotel.

'Where have you been?'

'Just down to the beach and for a mosey across the road.'

'That's a no-no. You have to radio me every time you leave the hotel or go to the pool and then I have to get clearance from the producers.'

F**k me. This was going to be a long week. On the second day, bored, I picked up the phone next to the bed to check if there was a dialling tone. There was, even though it was supposed to have been disconnected. No harm in giving it a go, I thought. So I dialled Michaela's number, fully expecting three security guards to come crashing through the hotel room door.

'Michaela, it's me,' I whispered when she answered. 'They've forgotten to disconnect my room phone!'

'Oh my god,' she said, bursting into tears again. 'How are you? Where are you? I can tell you who some of the other contestants are . . .'

'No, no, no – don't tell me. I don't want to know. If there's someone I hate, I won't sleep for the next few nights.'

'Well, there's someone there I think you will have a laugh with,' she said.

We spoke to each other every day for the rest of the week, but I was adamant that I didn't want to know about any other contestants. The only one I had an inkling about was Gemma Collins from reality show *The Only Way Is Essex*, because one of the kids' hairdressers had been told.

When the crunch time arrived to start filming, I was unbelievably nervous. I'd been out of the limelight for a while and wasn't comfortable with so many TV cameras in my face. The other celebrities would probably be used to all that. When I walked into the villa, Craig Charles from

Coronation Street was already there and it was nice when he said: 'Hey, Foggy! I'm glad you're in here.' I knew him because *Corrie* seems to be on our TVs at home every night of the week. Then came two contestants who I didn't recognise – Vicky Michelle from *'Allo 'Allo!* and Nadia Forde, an Irish singer and model – and finally Gemma Collins. They were all entertainers, all so at home in front of the cameras. That made me even more nervous, which I think came across on the first show. Then Dec, no Ant – I can never remember which one's which – anyway, the one with the big forehead, told us that the public had voted us into the Celebrity Slammer, a jungle jail, while the other group would spend another night in luxury, coincidentally at one of Mick Doohan's villas. I was so relieved. I just wanted to be in the jungle by that point.

My nerves soon disappeared when we jumped into a helicopter to take us from the Gold Coast up into camp. Gemma was in the front seat and was freaking out, because she was terrified of heights. 'Well, you must have known what you were letting yourself in for?' I thought. When the blades started up, she was screaming her head off and I couldn't control myself in the back seat. Everyone else was acting all concerned, which made it even funnier. Then she turned around and I could see that her make-up had run down her face. She looked like that Chucky doll from the horror movie *Child's Play* – but melted. I completely lost it. 'Stop it, Carl,' said Nadia, digging me in the ribs and trying not to laugh herself. 'It's not funny!' That just set me off again.

They had to get Gemma out of the helicopter, but the rest of us were dumped in the middle of the jungle and made to trek to camp. On the way, we had to go down a zip-wire ride in the pitch black. Craig went first and we could hear a little whoosh, then a snapping sound, then nothing. 'F**k me, something's gone wrong and he's plunged to his death,' I thought. And that set me off laughing again. It was just nervous laughter but it set Nadia off, too. Why were we laughing if something terrible might have happened? A few seconds later, we heard a cry of 'That was awesome!' from somewhere down below. Phew.

After that the guides took the wrong turn and we were lost in the middle of the jungle in the middle of our first night. We hadn't even started the challenges yet. The producers finally radioed for a minivan to pick us up and, by my reckoning, we made it into camp at around 1 am. I tried to ask one of the security guards for the time, but his watch face was taped up and his mouth might well have been, too, because he wasn't going to respond. Shit, these guys were taking this stuff seriously. After lighting the fire with a flint, I couldn't sleep. It was so hot and my mind was racing. Gemma trooped in about an hour later, woke everyone else up and then started snoring like a camel in labour.

I hardly slept a wink that first night, and the first day in the Slammer was a nightmare for me. I felt panicky and out of breath, thinking: 'What the hell are you doing here? What have you done?' In the next breath, I was telling myself: 'Come on, Carl, get a grip. You are mentally strong enough to do this.'

It took me back to the only time when I showed signs of weakness before a race, on the morning of my third world title win at Sugo in Japan in 1998. It didn't help that I had run over the head of a Japanese rider in the warm-up when he crashed in front of me. He was okay, but it freaked me out. Troy Corser was leading the championship so the pressure was on him more than me, although I was confident I'd be able to claw back the difference over two races, because Troy was not that fast at Sugo. Then he crashed badly in morning warm-up and ruptured his spleen. All of a sudden, the pressure was back on me and, when I heard 'Three Lions (Football's Coming Home)' by Baddiel & Skinner & the Lightning Seeds playing in the garage, I fell apart like a cheap watch. Michaela had to bring James over to calm me down. I managed to dig deep in the first race to finish third and leapfrog Aaron Slight into the championship lead by two points. Troy was out of action, so I just needed to beat Slight in race two and I had the title in the bag. With 10 laps to go the bike started to judder and vibrate as if a chunk had come out of the rear tyre, but I was well ahead of Slight and managed to nurse it home – a huge relief after two years without a world title.

But here, in the middle of the Australian jungle, I didn't have Michaela or James to help me out. I didn't want to say anything to the other contestants, so there were only the guys in the Bush Telegraph to speak to. Luckily, that night, it was the guy who'd already told me he was a big fan who used to follow my career. 'It's probably just the shock of the new surroundings,' he told me.

'No, it's more than that. I feel really panicky. I might have to get out of here,' I said.

They gave me a couple of pills and, as the day went on, I did start to calm down. Only I know just how close I was to walking out on the first day.

Then the Slammer phone rang and Craig said: 'Foggy, pack your things. You're heading off.' 'But I don't want to go,' I thought. 'I'm just settling down. What the hell's going on?' My head was mangled all over again. The guy who was waiting for me in the van said the other campmates had voted me to do the first challenge. 'Why me? Do they not like me? I haven't done anything wrong – yet.' All these thoughts were running through my head, with me not realising that the other camp had voted for the person they thought was most likely to win food for them. Mel Sykes, who presented MotoGP, had really pushed for me. The footballer Jimmy Bullard did too, but only after he realised I wasn't the film star, Owen Wilson.

I was led out of the van to meet Ant and Dec, who I'd not had the chance to speak to yet. Here were these two TV legends and here I was, a gibbering wreck. I was in a complete daze and they could have asked me to do anything. If they had told me to stand there naked and be kicked repeatedly in the bollocks by a mule, I would have done it. As it was, I had to lie in a pit of snakes. Piece of piss. Dr Bob gave me the talk about them not being poisonous but warned they would bite if they felt threatened. 'Am I supposed to act scared?' I wondered, as the snakes were dropped into the pit. I wasn't bothered in the slightest and started singing Oasis songs to pass the time. I smashed the trial and was interviewed afterwards by Ant and Dec when I felt a movement in my shorts. 'F**k me, this is embarrassing,' I thought. 'I'm getting a hard-on on live TV from talking to Ant and Dec.' Then I realised there was still a snake up there. The boys took a step back and the zoologist woman rushed in and stuck her hand up. 'Make sure you grab the right snake, girl,' I said and Ant and Dec both laughed. What a relief. I could be funny after all.

There was no question, when I was given a choice, that the food was following me to my new camp, and not going back to the Slammer. It wasn't malicious, just that this was the reason these other guys had picked me. As I wandered down the track into the main camp, I passed this old dude coming the other way, but he just ignored me. 'Must be one of the staff,' I thought. It was actually Michael Buerk, the newsreader. Then I met Dizzee Rascal, or at least that's who I thought it was. 'I'm Foggy, you must be Dizzee,' I said.

'Nah, Tinchy Stryder, man,' he said.

'Why? Do you take small steps?'

'Eh?'

'Sorry, just trying to make a joke. Forget it. Look, there's an eagle!'

Perhaps I wasn't as funny as I thought. Then I met Mel and Jimmy and got a pleasant surprise when the final member of their camp was the former *Playboy* playmate, Kendra Wilkinson. I told her I had seen the show *The Girls of the Playboy Mansion*, then immediately realised that this might be going out on national television and that Michaela may just possibly not be aware that I watched it (just once, of course). Kendra was the best-looking and always getting into trouble. I liked that.

I clicked with Jimmy straightaway the next morning, after finally getting some sleep. He was scared stiff of anything that moved, so I took every chance to flick a cockroach at him, tickle his arse with a leafy branch in the shower, or pounce on him from behind a bush. He was so funny and really brought me out of my shell. But he was constantly jabbering on about food, which made it worse. I actually didn't mind the rice and beans, and I told myself to think about all the people around the world who were starving to death.

I quickly settled into the role of camp provider. I wanted to keep busy, collecting firewood, boiling the water or keeping the fire going. I also tried to look after the girls whenever I could; I think it's a lot tougher for women in there. Nadia – or, as I called her, Princess Nala, from *The Lion King* – struggled with the food situation and one night begged me for a bit of the chocolate brownie I had won in a Dingo Dollar challenge. There was nobody more surprised than me when I let her have it. 'What's going on? I'm not supposed to be nice.' Then Vicky was really missing her mascara. When I noticed that the flame from the oil lanterns left soot on the inside of the glass, I suggested that she smeared some around her eyes. It worked a treat, so we made a little brush out of a stick and she did this every day. She was made up, literally.

Within a couple of days, we were back down to eight campmates. Craig had to leave due to the death of his brother, which was a shame because I think we would have got on. I don't think he would have taken any prisoners. Then Gemma said she'd had enough of the hunger. I didn't mind her, either. She was loud and outspoken, but she could laugh at herself and that's a big tick with me. 'So, I'm coping with the lack of food, keeping myself busy, and I'm getting on with the other celebrities. Those were my three main worries. Maybe this wasn't such a bad idea after all,' I thought. But it was obvious there would be a couple of new additions. And I don't usually like change.

FOGGY PHENOMENA
10 songs

Oasis – 'Live Forever'

Would this be my funeral song?

The Killers – 'Smile Like you Mean it'

Reminds me of the Petronas years.

Blondie – 'Heart of Glass'

Debbie Harry was my first boyhood crush. Can't think why.

My Chemical Romance – 'Black Parade'

Sends shivers down the back of my neck – especially when the coffin shuts in the video.

Suede – 'Trash'

This is mine and Michaela's theme tune. That Britpop era was awesome.

Coldplay – 'Fix You'

Always makes my hairs stand on end.

Echo and the Bunnymen – 'Nothing Lasts Forever'

This was my song in the jungle because every day was so long. Then Jimmy started to copy me, so I stopped.

Meat Loaf – 'Bat out of Hell'

Faster than any other boy has ever gone. Remind you of anyone?

Green Day – 'American Idiot'

Dedicated to John, Scott and Colin . . . Just kidding.

Joy Division – 'Love Will Tear Us Apart'

Memories of being a reckless teenager with my Harrington jacket and Docs.

KING CARL II

I was convinced that Jake Quickenden was gay when this strapping lad bounded into camp, with Edwina Currie in tow. Within an hour he was lying on top of Kendra, spooning with Mel and flirting with Nadia. So I'd obviously got that one wrong.

I was the last person he introduced himself to, and he told me that his dad had been a fan and had once told him about my reputation for speaking my mind. He'd also read some comments I made before the show about taking no nonsense off other celebrities, so I think he was a bit wary of me at first. Back at home in England, just before they set off for Australia, Michaela and the girls took a bit of a dislike to him because the producers were making it look like he'd broken up the 'bromance' between me and Jimmy. He was obviously a talented lad, who had just been voted off the *X Factor* finals after missing out at the Judge's House stage a couple of years earlier when Nicole Scherzinger sent him home. He'd had a tough time, too, losing his dad and then his brother to cancer. You can only admire someone who bounces back from that and tries to make something of himself.

I liked Edwina straightaway, too. She's a tough old bird who says it as she sees it. All I knew of her career was that she'd almost put the country's chicken farmers out of business with some comments about salmonella in eggs. And that she'd shagged John Major. I was dying to ask her about the John Major bit but decided against it. But I did love listening to her stories and I admired what she'd achieved. I'm usually a Tory voter, although I'm not into politics and couldn't tell you much about their policies. I just look at who's running for Prime Minister and decide who can best represent our country in a room full of other leaders. I'm sorry, but that Labour idiot, Corbyn, is never going to be able to do that. And I'm not sure Theresa May can, either. I'm looking for someone with stature, like David Cameron. I thought he could hold his own on the international stage. And I did vote for Tony Blair for the same reason in 1997.

Instead of Theresa May we should give Boris Johnson a go, just for the fun of it. Anyone who can get away with sending a 10-year-old Japanese kid flying with a rugby tackle or tackling one of the German players head first in a charity football match, gets my vote. Can you imagine the future of the planet in the hands of Boris and Donald Trump? What could possibly go wrong? I don't mind Trump, either. He was elected fair and square, so why not give him the chance to do things differently? Give him four years to see what he can achieve and judge him on that, instead of bitching and moaning about every single decision. You never ever hear the opposition say: 'What an excellent idea, we wish we had thought of that.'

Instead, they will always say there is some way the money could be spent better. It's a bit like racing. You never hear the guy who comes second saying that the winner is a better rider. There's always some excuse, like a problem with the bike. The only time I've ever heard a rider come close to admitting that was Troy Corser after my last double win at Assen in 1999, when he said there was nothing he could have done to beat me on that day, on that bike and on that circuit. I really respected him for saying that.

Back on politics, it's a shame Ed Balls never became Prime Minister. Imagine if he had to meet with the US president to discuss some plot against the two countries. It would have been like the Biggus Dickus scene from Monty Python's *Life of Brian* when nobody can take Pontius Pilate seriously. Balls even sounds a bit like him.

'Something smells off, Trump.' A few of the staff in the White House start to snigger.

'That's how I feel, Balls.' Most of the room is giggling now.

'I have a nose for this, Trump.' All the diplomats are trying hard not to laugh.

'Good, Ed. That's really good, Ed.' Now everyone's on the floor in stitches.

While we're at it, I'm all for Brexit, too. We have always been great on our own – it's *Great* Britain, after all. We're an island, surrounded by water, and not part of the Continent. I've never felt that welcome in Europe anyway, only by those people who recognise me from racing. We've probably kept several countries afloat with our tourism, so why should we keep propping them up? Let's start standing up for our farmers and our fishermen again. Let's regain control of our borders. And let's turn round to Europe and spell it out, quite clearly: 'The majority of our people have voted to leave Europe. You want how much money? Well, this is what you are getting. (Two fingers.) See ya.' Bollocks to all this Hard Brexit and Soft Brexit shit. Why can't we just leave and be done with it?

How the hell did I get into all that? Oh yes, Edwina Currie. I actually missed the one big fight in the jungle between Kendra and Edwina, because I was away doing a challenge with Jimmy, when he excelled himself at being a pussy in the Shed of Dread. Kendra was always willing to open up about her life inside the Playboy mansion and the problems she'd had with drug addiction as a teenager. Edwina was never short of an opinion and Kendra took real offence at her comments. Luckily, Kendra was always up for some banter with me and Jimmy.

One day, she was telling us about a sex-tape that was released by an ex-boyfriend. It was all getting very serious and I wasn't sure how to react, until Jimmy piped up: 'So, when he was filming, did he use a tripod or a handheld camera?' I fell off my camp bed laughing, but Kendra didn't understand the question at first.

'Well, what angle did he shoot from? How did he keep the camera steady? And did you film it all in one take, or did you have to keep stopping and starting?' We were both in hysterics.

'You're just a couple of dirty bastards,' she laughed. 'I'm not saying another word.'

For your information, Jimmy, it was mainly handheld – or so I'm told! I liked Kendra a lot. She's a real lad's girl. There was just one problem. She stank so bad that the rats hung around the dunny for some fresh air. It was disgusting, but she found it funny. She wasn't the slightest bit embarrassed. I was taking the piss about it one day when she picked up my pillow and rubbed it under her armpit. I was really pissed off and it took days to wash the stench out.

Jimmy sometimes walked a fine line with his banter. He liked to wind people up, but never quite knew when to quit. I think he actually struggled in there, especially with the lack of food. It was probably hard work being the camp clown 24 hours a day when you are so low on energy.

One morning, he had a bit of a go at me. 'F**kin' motorbike racer? Call that a sport? Anyone can ride a f**kin' motorbike, can't they?' he said.

'Says the man who reached his peak playing for Wigan. Look, I'm not taking you on. Say another thing and I'll just knock you out when we leave here,' I laughed.

Half an hour later he turned on Jake, who was laughing because Vicky had mistaken Jimmy for Michael Buerk, a man with the frame of Mr Burns from *The Simpsons*. Jimmy was not amused.

'I'm askin' myself what the f**k is this p***k doing here. What's he offering? What sort of skill has he got?' Jimmy ranted.

'Whoa! Calm down,' I thought to myself.

'I don't know why I'm here myself,' Jake replied, and he was obviously a bit put out. Jimmy realised he'd overstepped the mark and tried to laugh it off as banter. He even said: 'I shouldn't have said that. I can see it hurt ya.'

This was just before the camp was split into two teams to compete for immunity from the first public vote. Our team lost a few challenges, including when Edwina supposedly beat me in a trial of concentration and endurance. We had to keep our finger on a buzzer while being spun around on a platform as jungle critters dropped on our heads. I swear to this day that my finger did not leave that buzzer and knew I would be in for a lot of stick back home for being beaten by Edwina Currie. It also meant that the other team could select one of us to join them and they tactically chose Michael, thinking that if they lost the overall challenge then he might be first to be voted out.

But, thanks to another incredible show of bravery from Jimmy, we lost. He shouted 'I'm a Celebrity Get Me Out of Here!' about 10 seconds after being placed in a tomb with a couple of rats and came running out like Road Runner, his legs barely touching the ground. 'I'm a soft twat, get me out of here,' I laughed. But instead of staying in the clearing in front of the cameras, he ran straight into the jungle, which contained more scary stuff than inside the tomb. This meant that me, Jimmy, Mel and Tinchy were up for the first vote – four strong characters.

'Well, that's the end of that,' I thought, 'I've no chance.' Tinchy had about a million followers on Twitter, Jimmy must have been favourite to win the show because he was hilarious at times, and Mel would have strong daytime TV and male followings.

'Foggy ...' said Ant, or Dec, no I think it was Ant, during the first live vote-off, 'it's not you.' I could not believe what I was hearing. Mel had already been told she was safe and Tinchy was an 'it might be you'. So the other person in the bottom two was Jimmy. I just put my head in my hands. I couldn't believe that the public had voted to keep me safe. I'd already started to well up before hearing the result, which I was sure was going to be Tinchy, who was a good lad but quite quiet around camp. I nearly fell off the bench when Jimmy's name was read out. He'd kept me going through those first two weeks, but he was unpredictable. When he was good, he was buzzing. But when he was down, he could be a bit annoying. And the viewers had seen a different side to him during that argument with Jake. It's all in the editing, of course, and apparently it came across as bullying, not banter. There was no big fallout, although it was a bit uncomfortable at the time.

Having survived that scare, I was pretty sure I would be okay for the next few votes. Jimmy's departure meant I could relax a bit more, instead of being part of a double-act all the time. It helped my relationship with Jake, too. He was the life and the soul of the place and it was impossible not to like him, even though I thought he was lazy and had to be asked to do any chores, like emptying the dunny, which was foul. I started to really enjoy my time there. Obviously, I missed Michaela and the girls, but knew they would be enjoying themselves in the Versace hotel. I had actually seen Michaela briefly as part of one of the challenges, when she was allowed into a Pool Party that me, Vicky and Jimmy had been chosen for. We had ice lollies on tap and I must have had 10 in an hour, which gave me the runs – unlike Jimmy, who had one shit in the two weeks he was there and, even then, all that came out were two tiny sheep pellets.

Michaela told me that everyone was loving me back home but couldn't say a lot more because she was told not to tell us anything about the outside world, not even whether Lewis Hamilton had won the world championship! But she did tell me that I stank of campfire smoke, that I'd lost weight and that my eyes looked really clear. Apparently, that's something which happens quite often because you are not eating preservatives and all that shit.

'I've got a bit of a semi-on,' I said as we had a brief hug and kiss before she was about to go.

'Get off me you dirty bastard, I'm off,' she laughed, and disappeared back into the bushes.

We also received luxury items from home on one show and mine was a picture of Michaela and the girls, which I pinned up next to my bed. Jake clocked this and said: 'Blondie looks a bit of alright.'

'You've no chance,' I said. 'Danielle's really picky with men.' How wrong could I be!?

One by one the other contestants were voted off and I found myself in the final three. This was better than I could have hoped for and I resigned myself to coming third. There was no way I would beat ITV's golden girl, Mel, and this big likeable hunk, Jake. But before the final day, there was one final challenge and I was convinced that I would be given the eating challenge. I'd already survived one drinking challenge, although the half a pint of warm deer's blood was the most disgusting stuff you could imagine. The animal's heart and liver were blended with crunchy eyeballs and it stank like . . . well, Kendra, come to think of it. I gulped it down, but the blood stuck to my mouth and looked like bright red lipstick.

'F**kin' 'ell,' shouted Jimmy. 'It's only Edwina on a night out!'

My guts started doing somersaults even before I left the set, but Dr Bob told me to try and keep it down. 'That's 85 per cent protein and the most nutritious stuff you've had in here,' he said. 'It's better than a fillet steak for protein.' It certainly didn't taste better.

For the final Bush Tucker Trial, they try to tempt you not to win food for the final dinner in camp that night by showing you a 'tasty' alternative. But I would have rather had live cockroaches than the soggy pizza they offered. So instead, I first had to eat a full tankard of mealworms. I'm sure that in past series contestants only had to eat one or two, not a full tankard. I tried to crunch them up as quickly as possible so that they were not wriggling inside my mouth and were all dead before swallowing. 'If that was a starter, what's coming next?' I wondered. But the mealworm course was actually the worst of the lot, and the next four challenges were a breeze. The fried tarantulas were soft on the inside but crunchy on the outside – like dog shit wrapped in Kentucky, as I described it on air. Next up were two live cockroaches, but the hardest bit was catching one of them. Then there was an ostrich anus from the ostrich with the hairiest arsehole in Australia. Finally, I had to chew the end of a camel's bell-end – and not many people say that in life and get away with it. I know some people complain about the eating challenges. That's a load of bollocks. To moan that live insects are being eaten for entertainment, when millions of cows, chickens and pigs are being slaughtered every day for food, is so hypocritical.

The final morning in camp was very emotional. I'd grown attached to this beautiful place and was going to miss it. One of the other campmates had asked me where I saw myself in five years' time and I said: 'Sat right here on my camp bed having failed to readjust to life in the outside world.' It wasn't just the jungle that had an effect on me. I loved being on the show, too. You have no energy in there, but you adapt to that. And there were no Billy Big Bollocks among the celebrities, because I might have struggled if there had been. Everyone was down to earth and fun to be around. I probably didn't gel with Michael as much as the others and, when he was voted off, I jokingly asked what he did for a living. But, to give him credit, Michael did pull his weight around camp. And I could already tell that being on the show would change me as a person. I felt more comfortable in my own skin and more confident around strangers.

There was nothing much to do on the final morning. (They even sneaked a bacon butty in for us, but don't tell anyone. And I can assure you here and now that there were no other treats, although I did manage to nick a couple of small bananas out of the backpack of one of the staff when he wasn't looking. It was out of sight of the cameras, but somebody monitoring the microphones must have wondered what we were all giggling at.) Then it was time for the final three – me, Jake and Mel – to go to meet Ant and Dec. I was so happy with third place.

'Whoa! Mel just got voted off. What the hell happened there? I'm in the top two. F**k me sideways, I'm in the final of the biggest show on British television!' I looked at Jake, who was just as stunned as me. After what seemed like 20 minutes, we were led up towards the main studio area and then everything became a blur again. I could see Ant and Dec, all the crew, all the other contestants, all the cameras. I tried looking for Michaela and the girls but couldn't see them. There was a glass of champagne waiting, and the first sip of that went straight to my head. Then it was time to announce the winner. Kian Egan from Westlife, the previous year's winner, was waiting with the big wooden sceptre in his hand.

'And the winner of *I'm a Celebrity . . . Get Me Out of Here!* 2014 and the new King of the Jungle is . . .'

'I think they're going to say my name . . .' I thought.

'. . . Foggy!'

I just dropped to my knees like I'd been shot in the head. The fireworks went off, they put the laurel crown on my head, the campmates were cheering, Kian gave me the sceptre and then I was told to 'Get Yourself Out of Here!' As soon as I was on the bridge, I spotted Michaela and the girls going ballistic on the other side and I dropped to my knees again for the cameras before Michaela came running on and nearly knocked me over the side.

'Oh My God. I'm so sorry,' she bawled. 'I'm so sorry I ever doubted you.' Claudia and Danielle were in floods of tears. It was just too much to take in – all I wanted was to get back to the hotel and have a bath. But everyone wanted a piece of me and the rest of the day was just crazy.

I remember someone trying to take the sceptre off me. 'What, I don't get to keep it?' I asked. 'No, it's impossible for you to take back in your checked-in luggage and they wouldn't allow it in hand luggage,' the producer explained.

Joe Swash, who presented the ITV2 show, heard this and snatched the sceptre out of my hand. Then he snapped it in two over his knee. 'It'll fit in his luggage now,' he grinned.

The journey back to the Versace hotel seemed to take a lifetime and we stopped at the side of the road for ages, waiting for the bus with the other celebrities plus their friends and families to overtake us because they are traditionally supposed to cheer the winner into the hotel. Apparently, Edwina had an upset tummy and stopped the bus so that she could crouch at the edge of a sugarcane field. Dr Bob was called from camp and it took a while to sort her out.

My manager Neil, who lives in Australia now, was back at the hotel. He'd been up on the Gold Coast for a couple of weeks, running my social media and liaising with the British newspapers. He was bawling his eyes out, too. Back in the room, I grabbed anything I could get my hands on to eat. I'd been warned not to do this, and I suffered an hour or so later. But I needed some energy to make it through the endless interviews.

The sceptre was repaired in time for a live interview on the *Lorraine* show the following morning UK time, tea-time in Australia, but I still managed to sneak it back to our room at the Versace and hide it in the luggage, prompting the biggest security operation since Versace himself was shot. By the time of the after-show party I was running on empty, although I was expected to attend and the kids were looking forward to it. All the friends and family had bonded well and my mob had made good friends with Jimmy's manager, Jim Erwood, as well as Jake's mum, Lisa.

We joined everyone in the minibus taking us to the nightclub at the other end of the Gold Coast, but it looked like Jimmy had been partying for the whole week that he had been out. He got it in his head that the bus driver looked like Jimmy Savile, although he actually looked nothing like him.

'Oi, Savile, get a f**kin' move on,' he shouted, staggering up and down the aisle. Then he said something to Jake's mum and Jake was ready to knock his block off. One of the producers had to intervene and threatened to throw Jimmy off the bus unless he sat down and shut up. He sat down but didn't shut up until we got there. That's Jimmy – sometimes you need an off-switch.

The party was the final straw for me and I only lasted for about half an hour, time enough to thank all the crew and put a name to the faces in the Bush Telegraph at last. Ant and then Dec – or was it Dec and then Ant – came over to congratulate me. Then we snuck out back to the hotel and passed the reporters waiting in the foyer, who I couldn't speak to because I'd signed an exclusive deal with one of the national newspapers. Finally, I jumped onto a comfy bed for a good night's sleep. Except my mind was still racing. I was trying to make sense of it all. It turned out later that, apart from that first vote-off, I won every night's phone vote. It was a massive show of support from all my fans and probably a lot of new ones, who liked the Foggy they saw on their television screens. I said in some of the first interviews that it was the best thing that had ever happened to me, and I got some stick for that – quite rightly. My world championship wins were more important, obviously. It was said in the heat of the moment.

This was different kind of win though, an intensely personal victory. Okay, it's just a TV show. But it's probably the biggest and the best, with 13 million people watching every night, every year. And for a few weeks it's your whole life, nothing else matters. So to conquer my personal demons and prove to myself and my family that I can, as Mark told me to, embrace who I am – well, it's certainly one of my proudest achievements.

FOGGY PHENOMENA
10 career moments

First TT win

The 750cc class in 1989. I'd wanted a TT win since watching my dad as a young kid.

Brands Hatch, 1995

The perfect day. Two controlled wins to complete the double-double on home circuits.

Donington, 1992

My first WSBK victory. As a privateer, too. I had arrived . . .

Assen

Pick any race from my 12 wins. This was my patch.

Senior TT, 1992

Although I lost the Race of the Century with Hizzy, I broke the lap record on a bike that was falling to bits.

Le Mans 24 Hours, 1992

Such a shock to the system, but amazing to win my first 24-hour race.

MBE

Always been very proud of this honour.

Phillip Island, 1994

The first WSBK title was always the most special.

1990 TT

With wins in the Senior and Formula One, I was now a road racer to be reckoned with.

I'm a Celebrity

Arguably my hardest victory.

15

It was sad to say goodbye to everyone and head straight back to the UK and the madness that was waiting for me there. It was the busiest few weeks of my life, although I did manage to see a few campmates on various TV shows in the run-up to Christmas. Then Jake turned up at our house. 'It's nice that he wants to keep in touch with me,' I thought. I'm a bit slow on the uptake with stuff like that. Jake and Danielle had got chatting at the after-show party in Australia and stayed in touch. So, although he said he was 'just in the area' and 'fancied dropping by', there was possibly an ulterior motive.

Danielle had only ever had one serious boyfriend and didn't trust celebrities or footballers. She's quite switched on like that. And I was quite protective of the girls at first, because a dad knows what lads are like. Then we worried whether she would ever find the right person. But soon they were dating officially, next they were on *This Morning* talking about it, then Jake was moving into Danielle's house in Manchester and, boom, they were engaged. Now I'm saving up for the wedding, so I was praying that he won *Dancing on Ice* and could contribute!

We are lucky that both Claudia and Danielle are a credit to us, and we have kept their feet on the ground. I was actually quite hands on with the girls when they were young and didn't shy away from changing nappies in the motorhome during a race weekend, although Michaela would be the one to get up with them in the middle of the night before a race. I took them to school whenever I was around and tried to help with the homework but, as girls start to grow up, the mum is the more influential figure. It's the same with lads and their dads. We let them go off and make their own mistakes when the time was right, and neither of them are the type to go out partying every night. Danielle works at a Pilates studio in Alderley Edge but isn't quite as career-minded as Claudia, who is a partner in a drama and singing company called Little Voices and is doing really well.

I love to wind Claudia up and one recent prank came off a treat when she asked me to book some Ryanair flights for her and a group of friends. Just before clicking 'Confirm' you are offered every add-on imaginable: an inflatable dinghy; life insurance; cheap funerals; and in-flight meals. Nobody, and I mean nobody, has ever pre-ordered an in-flight meal on Ryanair, or on any other airline for that matter. So, imagine Claudia's horror when, half an hour after take-off, the stewardess arrived with not one, but two full English breakfasts.

'But I didn't order anything,' she pleaded.

'Yes, you did,' said the stewardess at the top of her voice. 'Two full

English breakfasts for Claudia Fogarty in seat 6F. Is that you? Well, here you are. Two full English breakfasts.'

The other passengers were all thinking: 'What a greedy cow. Is one breakfast not enough?' Especially when she peeled back one of the foil lids and everyone could smell the disgusting scrambled eggs. 'How can she eat two lots of that shit?' the other passengers must have been asking themselves. Claudia had never been so embarrassed in her life. It was the best £120, or whatever Ryanair charge for two full English breakfasts, I'd ever spent.

Jake became part of the furniture at our house in no time, as Danielle is quite a home bird and they spend most of their weekends with us. And, just like in the jungle, he leaves the place looking like a bomb has hit it. After a Jake visit, there is no beer or red wine in the house and there are half-finished cans of Coke everywhere. That drives me up the wall – and it's not just Jake. Kids open a drink, have one sip and then just leave it. Either A) Finish the whole bottle; B) Don't open it in the first place if you don't really want it; C) Pour it away so I can't find it; or D) Buy your own bloody drinks and you can do whatever you want with them.

Seriously, though, Jake's a good lad and more like a mate than a prospective son-in-law. It would have been easy for him to go off the rails after what he has been through, but he works hard, especially on social media – maybe a little too hard, in my opinion. There are times when you just have to ignore someone who has had a pop. They are only doing it for the reaction. It's the proudest moment of their life to go down the pub and tell their mates: 'I've just called Wayne Rooney a wanker on Twitter.' Round of applause to the genius who invented social media. You have created a way for people who have achieved absolutely nothing in life to have a direct go at someone who has. It used to wind me up, too, but I have calmed down with social media now. I try to make my posts light-hearted by taking the piss out of myself.

Some messages from followers can be confusing, so it's best to ignore them. Like the time I received a message from someone who I didn't know saying, 'I always thought you were . . .' with a winking emoticon. Eh? What's all that about? Then I looked again. It was in response to a tweet I had supposedly sent out saying, 'I am gay'. I knew immediately what had happened. I'd made the schoolboy error of leaving my phone unguarded with Claudia in the house. She thought it was hilarious until I went mental. It was in my early days on Twitter, so I didn't know how to delete it and had to wait for Neil to get into my account. By that time the comments had started to flood in. Luckily, I didn't have too many follow-ers at that time.

You also have to be careful on social media, because it's easy to post something that might have been better worded or could be taken out of context. That happened to me when Valentino Rossi unfollowed me on Twitter after I made a comment about the Rossi-Marquez incident at Sepang towards the end of the epic MotoGP season in 2015. Rossi had accused Marquez of holding him up at Phillip Island to allow Jorge Lorenzo to score as many points as possible and extend his lead over Rossi. But if that had been the case, wouldn't Marquez have let Lorenzo win the race? He didn't, and Marquez came through right at the end to take victory.

'From Phillip Island, it's clear that Jorge has a new fan. Marc has played with us, doing everything in Lorenzo's advantage,' Rossi said the following week at the press conference just before the race in Sepang. You could sense at that stage that he was losing the plot a bit. Rossi was probably realising that his rides in the wet, including his win at the British GP, had kept his title hopes alive and that he was struggling to keep up with Marquez and Lorenzo in the dry. He was frustrated, and it showed at Sepang when, after knocking paint off each other for about three laps, Rossi forced Marquez out wide and appeared to kick out, causing Marquez to crash. It was the most un-Rossi-like thing I had ever seen. This was one of the greatest riders in the history of the sport, if not the greatest. I couldn't have any more respect for the guy. But it was sad to see him so frustrated – and so reckless. Usually, he would have done his talking on the track. I tweeted something along the lines of: 'That one stupid act has ruined an amazing career.' Then I suggested Rossi and Marquez should go back out for a two-lap shoot-out to settle it. And finally, a bit later, I tweeted: 'Think if it had been any other rider they would of been disqualified from the race for sure #justsaying #MotoGP' (including the little halo emoticon).

I had set the cat among the pigeons and got a torrent of abuse on Twitter from Rossi fans:

'F**k off back to the jungle!' @ilovemeatpies, aged 55, Grimsby.

'Excuse me? Who are you?' @azizaziraziz, aged 12, Indonesia.

'Don't you mean "have" and not "of"?' @ipolicegrammar, aged 83, Eton.

'Didn't you once try to knock me off?' @realjohnkocinski, 50, Arkansas. (Not that real!)

I wouldn't mind, but most Rossi fans don't know anything about racing – I think most of them just like the colour yellow! In truth, I was probably a bit hungover from a Saturday night out when I sent that first tweet in the early hours of Sunday morning. I should have waited a bit and tweeted a more considered opinion. I deleted the first tweet a few days later but the damage had been done and I wish I hadn't said it. But when all is said and done, it did look like Rossi was trying to knock Marquez off. And you can't do that. I'm speaking from experience because it's correct, I did try to knock John Kocinski off once. It was the most reckless thing I've ever done on a race track. And another thing I really regret.

It was during the second race at A1 Ring in Austria in 1997, a season when I rode the Ducati hard but Kocinski's Honda was a lot faster. I went into that round frustrated by my own incompetence at Brands Hatch in the previous round. I threw crucial points away by crashing in the first race by being too impatient because two riders, including Kocinski in the lead, were holding me up. I won the second race, which was split into two because of the wet conditions. It was possibly my best ever ride in the wet, but I did receive an official warning from the FIM for riding too dangerously when Frankie Chili's bar clipped my back end as I came underneath him. I didn't even know he had gone down and Chili admitted that he was partly responsible for the crash because he hadn't lifted his bike up enough. I admit I was riding aggressively and sometimes dangerously that year, but not on that occasion.

In Austria, I managed to keep the winning streak going in the first race, again by riding on the edge. I was leading the second race, too, but Kocinski kept passing me on the straight because his bike was quicker. So I always had to out-brake him into the hairpin. It was so frustrating, and the red mist descended. This was a rider I did not like, to put it mildly. I felt he was a real oddball and thought he probably suffered from Obsessive Compulsive

Disorder. Me and James used to park our motorhomes directly opposite him so that we could spy on what he was up to. We once spotted him spend half an hour washing a bunch of car keys outside his motorhome – he was obsessed with cleanliness. I just wish I'd had the balls to sneak into his motorhome and switch his Hoover from suck to blow. He also liked to have his gloves, helmet, bananas and water bottle lined up perfectly on the table in his garage and, when Neil Hodgson was his team-mate, Neil found himself alone in the garage before a practice session. It was a golden opportunity, so he messed up everything on the table, chucked the bananas on the floor and then sat back to watch the mayhem when Kocinski arrived in the garage and tried to find the culprit.

Things had also kicked off in the media that year when I called Kocinski a 'freak of nature'. That was how I was back then! So, when he took the lead in that race at the A1 Ring, I was ready to try anything to win. Going into the hairpin, I thought that I would let go of the brakes just as he was tipping in, so that I could clip his front wheel. He would probably go down and I would stay up. But I changed my mind at the last second and hit the brakes hard, clipping his back wheel. I went down but Kocinski just wobbled into the gravel and was able to re-join the race and regain the championship lead. Things were now going Kocinski's way. My winning streak at Assen was ended when the biggest bluebottle in Holland splattered into my visor and I couldn't see a bloody thing, although I bounced back to win the second race. Then the championship was all but lost when I crashed twice at Albacete, a track that I usually did so well at. It was one of the lowest points of my career.

I admit I should have been punished for that Austria incident, and it was right that Rossi was punished for the Sepang incident. It was just a joke how he was punished, though. He should have been disqualified from that race and his points deducted. That's what would have happened in F1. But, no, that would have meant Rossi couldn't have won the championship at the final round in Valencia. So, what did these geniuses say? 'Now, Mr Rossi. You have done something very dangerous on track. But instead of docking your points or fining you, we are going to create an even more dangerous situation by sticking you at the back of the grid at Valencia so that you might knock other riders off trying to charge through the field and win the race.' Rossi was never going to win in Valencia, but it was an example of the FIM at their most ridiculous.

There are always two side to any story, of course. That was the case with another notorious incident involving me and Frankie Chili at Assen in 1998. Things had been tense in the team all year because Davide Tardozzi was running me, while Virginio Ferrari was running a two-man team of Corser and Chili. I was paranoid that Chili, an Italian riding for an Italian manufacturer, was getting the best engines. I knew I needed to win both races at Assen to have any chance of the title and was furious when Chili breezed past me down the straight on the final lap to take the win. I needed to stop the same thing happening in race two and, on the final lap, weaved over to the other side of the track to stop him using the slipstream. We almost collided at the next left, when I let my bike run wide. Then he overtook when I missed a gear, but I knew I could out-brake him into the final chicane. I was so late on the brakes that my back end was weaving around and Chili tried to pass on the outside but lost his front end. I genuinely had no idea he'd crashed.

The 20,000 Brits went mental and it was only when I saw Chili marching towards me as I came back into pit-lane that I realised he'd crashed. He aimed a pathetic punch at me, which glanced off my visor. So I did a burn-out right in his face. He had to be pulled away but then turned up at the post-race press conference wearing a shabby blue dressing gown – not a good look. When the interviewer asked if there were any more questions from the floor, Chili stood up and said: 'What this man has done here today was a disgrace.'

'I'm not listening to this shit,' I said, standing up to leave. I had to walk past Chili and it all kicked off again – handbags at dawn. It's forgotten now and we always have a laugh whenever we meet up. But can you imagine what might have happened if Twitter had been around in those days? #nevertouchedya

FOGGY PHENOMENA
10 career downers

Formula One TT, 1992

Breaking down while in the lead by 35 seconds with just over a lap to go.

British GP, 1993

So close to a podium, until I started running out of fuel.

BBC Sports Personality of the Year

My name should have been on that trophy in 1999.

Laguna Seca, 1997

My one big chance to win at a circuit I usually struggled at was ruined by food poisoning.

World Superbikes, 1993

I would have won my first WSBK title without crashes at Donington and Sugo.

British GP, 1992

Crashed after touching coolant while running fifth with five laps to go.

Oulton Park, 1986

A crash on a practice day set my career back two years.

Brands Hatch, 1999

I felt at the time I let those 120,000 fans down.

Phillip Island, 2000

The day it all ended.

The Weakest Link

Still not recovered from the embarrassment!

16

TRAVEL SICKNESS

If it was sad to leave the jungle, it was even sadder to go back the following year to present the new King or Queen of the Jungle with their crown. It turned out to be Vicky Pattison from *Geordie Box*. She was followed by Scarlett Moffatt from *Goggle Shore* the following year, and then in 2017 it was Georgia Toffolo from *Made in Essex*, or whatever those shit reality shows are called. That's three Queens of the Jungle since I was there, so in my book I'm still the reigning King of the Jungle. It's sad, I know.

I appeared on the ITV2 show for a few nights before the final and that was fun. They also staged a piece around me in the jungle on a Triumph in the build-up to the Celebrity Cyclone with the other ITV2 presenters, Joe Swash and Laura Whitmore, which was also a good laugh. But I felt out of place being on the other side of the fence. We had been really looking forward to going back, but it wasn't even the same for Michaela. She had been so involved with everything when she was here with the girls and the other friends and families. They were looked after so well at the Versace and she was on the ITV2 show a couple of times herself. So she felt left out of things, too. Joe Swash, who also won the show, told me that he felt exactly the same – he missed the place so much and really struggled when he returned the following year. At dinner one evening, when I was telling Michaela and Neil about the details of life in the camp, I was so emotional that I almost burst into tears.

In the studio, where the ITV2 show is filmed and Ant and Dec present the main show, you are so close to the camp – too close for me. I genuinely wanted to be back in there. At the very least, after the winner had been announced and the camp was empty, I wanted to take Michaela to show her where my bed was and to try and give her a taste of the magic of the place. But their rules and regulations are so strict, probably all to do with health and safety again, that I wasn't even allowed a brief visit. We were staying right at the other end of the Gold Coast from the Versace, too, so we couldn't even mingle with that year's contestants. And you couldn't relax on the beach there, because there were reports of a pack of wild dingos roaming the area. After the warnings about the crocs, box jellies, spiders and snakes up near the Barrier Reef, I was convinced that everything in Australia wants to kill you. We couldn't wait to be on the flight home.

Not that I enjoy flying. I'm actually quite a nervous passenger. Someone once told me that the most dangerous part of a flight is the first 10 seconds after take-off. If something does go wrong, a pilot needs height to be able to sort it out. So you'll always see me counting up to four, five, six . . . then the rest really quickly. My thinking is that humans were not meant to leave the ground. If we were meant to fly, cavemen would have evolved wings. And I don't like someone else being in control. I'm not really claustrophobic, but when something's going fast, I like to be in the driver's seat. For example, there was talk once of me doing a few rounds of the Formula One Powerboat World Championship. I even went down to Southampton for a dry run, on the water, if you see what I mean. But the weather was so crap, and the harbour so choppy, that it wasn't safe to go out into open water. Just being crammed in next to the driver in this floating, stretched sports car, with a Perspex roof locking you in, made me a bit uncomfortable. It wasn't for me. The older you get, the pickier you are about the adrenaline-junkie stuff that you will take on. Something like the land speed record that Triumph have been attempting wouldn't appeal. After the age of 40, you realise that if something goes wrong there, it doesn't just hurt, it can be terminal. But ask me to strap myself on a tea-tray and hurl myself down the Cresta Run, or to jump in a bobsleigh with a bunch of Jamaican sprinters and, yeah, I'll give that kind of thing a go.

Also on my bucket list would be diving in a cage with sharks. Michaela tried to book it for my 40th birthday in South Africa but was told that they were stopping them because it was encouraging sharks to come closer to shore. Either that or she found a good excuse to pull out because of the cost. I'd have no problems being in a cage with a Great White trying to batter its way in for a gobful of Foggy flesh. I love all creatures that are top of the food chain.

Lions are amazing, although it would appear they don't feel the same about me. After the World Superbike round in South Africa in Kyalami in 1998, when I was second in both races behind Frankie Chili, we all headed out to a secure restaurant complex in a posh area of Johannesburg called

Sandton. James was riding for Suzuki and his wife, Andrea, was there with Michaela too, so it was guaranteed to be a lively night. Add to that lethal cocktail the fact that Corser was buying rounds of disgusting black shots every five minutes and it was a recipe for the worst hangover in history. Everyone spent the night spewing their guts up, but we'd all been booked to go on a mini-safari by the local Ducati dealers, so it seemed rude to back out. The track in the compound was hideously bumpy and I couldn't wait to stop and chuck up again. The only problem was that we were already inside the lion section. You wouldn't have known it because, instead of the electric fences and armed patrollers that we were expecting, there was one bloke with a bit of a twig to poke the lions with and keep them under control. I could hardly leap out of the car and risk becoming their afternoon snack, so all I could do was wind the window down, stick my head out and paint the side of the truck with my stomach contents. Instead of grabbing their chance for a kill, the lions just slowly got up and ambled off into the bushes, shaking their heads and tutting: 'Who's that dickhead? He stinks, I'm going nowhere near that shit.' The flight home later that evening was not the best.

It wasn't my worst flight, though. That would have to have been in the trustworthy hands of one James Whitham. It was another shoot for the *Hell for Leather III* DVD in 2011 and the plan was for me to go up in a two-seater light aircraft with James, who is a licensed pilot, or so he says, and actually runs his own airfield called Crosland Moor, near Huddersfield. The rich and the famous have landed there – the Queen, Tony Blair and Mick Jagger. There is a Portakabin for 'checking-in', or signing your name on a scrap of paper in this case, and a sign saying Huddersfield

International Airport Terminal 2. The sign for 'arrivals' reads: Ey up, Welcome, Bienvenue. The 'departures' sign reads: Taraa, Goodbye, Au Revoir. The departures 'lounge' consists of a stool and a kettle for making a brew. Now this flight in James' plane wouldn't have made for great DVD footage if I was a confident flyer. But I wasn't, so the humour was always going to come from my reaction, and there were cameras in the tiny cockpit to capture every grimace and squeal. It didn't help that it was blowing a gale up on the moors that day. At no point on that flight did I feel anything other than scared shitless. Then, after looking like we might land back-to-front at one point because we were being blown around so much as we approached the runway, I was finally able to scramble out of the cockpit to safety.

'Probably shouldn't have gone up today. Way too windy,' James said, cool as a cucumber. W**ker. James loves flying more than anyone in the world, but even he was as sick as a dog when he went up with the Red Arrows. Then he was gutted when he found out that I hadn't spewed when I did a publicity shoot with them once, along with Troy Corser and Suzi Perry. We all had to listen to a serious safety briefing and pass a medical, which I actually failed because I had a bad cold and couldn't do the lung function test properly. It was also quite soon after my crash in 2000, so I was still a bit all over the place in general. But the Commander let me off and we all climbed into our heavy-duty flying suits, complete with sick bags attached. Minutes into the flight we pulled alongside Suzi's plane and I looked across to give her the thumbs up, but she had her head in the bag, honking her guts up – although she denied it later. When my pilot did the equivalent of a hand-brake turn, the G-force was incredible and I could feel my cheeks being pushed down. I could barely lift my arms and wouldn't have been able to use the sick bag if I'd wanted to. As we came into land, he warned me that I'd feel wobbly and tired. Sure enough, my legs almost bucked when I climbed down onto the runway. And five minutes into the helicopter trip back home, I was sleeping like a baby.

I've actually got a soft spot for Huddersfield because the university, where Claudia also did her drama degree, awarded me an honorary degree for my services to motorbike racing in 2006. It was presented by actor Patrick Stewart from the *Star Trek* films, who was the Chancellor of the University. So I'm now an Honorary Doctor of Civil Law (DCL) and, if anyone wants a dispute settled, then I'm your man. My academic career didn't stop there, though. Years later, I was also awarded an Honorary Fellowship of the University of Central Lancashire. So my full title is now Carl Fogarty MBE, DCL. Not bad for a lad who left school without an O level to his name. You can have your own fun deciding what MBE, DCL might stand for – perhaps Massive Bell End, Doesn't Consider Losing.

Made-up letters after your name can be dangerous, though. Ask Steve Parrish, the former racer, turned TV pundit and, without question, the biggest joker on the motorbike circuit. His business cards read Steve Parrish, NLAMN, which stands for No Letters After My Name. Steve was once sitting comfortably in business class waiting for the flight back to London to leave Japan after the MotoGP race in Motegi in 2004. The cabin was full of bike-racing personalities but one of the air stewardesses noticed that John Hopkins, who had been involved in a pile-up caused by Loris Capirossi and suffered broken ribs and a deep cut as a result, was struggling to put his bag in the overhead locker. She called the dispatcher, who refused to let the flight take off with Hopkins in that condition. It was looking like they were going to miss their take-off slot, so up steps Parrish.

'Excuse me, I'm Dr Parrish. Here's my business card. You can see here, I'm an NLAMN – the circuit doctor. Can I be of assistance?'

The Japanese dispatcher was very impressed and, after watching a quick 'examination', accepted Steve's verdict that Hopkins was fit to travel. Dr Parrish even had to sign a waiver. Hopkins and the rest of the cabin kept schtum and the flight took off on time. Two hours away from London, the same flight attendant woke Steve up and said there was a problem with one of the passengers in cattle class. Would he mind examining them?

'Sure,' said Steve, making his way nervously to the back of the plane. He was almost on the brink of coming clean. When he got there the man was slumped in his chair, unconscious. 'My diagnosis is that this passenger is suffering from excess alcohol intake,' he said. 'Leave him to rest until we land, then give him a glass of water and two Paracetamol.' The 10 empty cans around his chair were a good clue. Good job they didn't ask him to deliver a baby, because he would probably have had a go.

Then there was another Parrish classic, on the way back from Daytona in 1995. This was a prestigious race back in the day and there was a big build-up in the local newspapers there about the rivalry between me and Scott Russell, and how much I hated the track – and all Americans, for that matter. That's not actually what I said, but the locals were out for my blood anyway. I was up with the leaders when Russell crashed early on and was illegally helped back onto his bike by the marshals. Then, after another small crash, the pace car came out without any real need. It was against the rules to pass another rider while the pace car was out, but I could see Russell weaving his way through the field without a care in the world. When he was back at the front, he was fast and I had to settle for second, but he should have been disqualified. There was no point Ducati appealing, though, as it wouldn't have got us anywhere with the biased American officials.

I needed cheering up on the way home, and there's nobody better to provide a laugh than Parrish. He often carries a scruffy piece of fur which looks like a black mouse, attached to a really thin fishing line. This is wound up on a coil mechanism in his pocket. When he hits the button, the mouse whizzes back towards his pocket. Everyone in the paddock was catching the same plane back from Miami, so Steve knew he had an audience at the tables outside an ice cream stall in the departures lounge. So he leant over the counter and dropped the mouse in a tub of raspberry ripple. Then, when the assistant was heading there to serve another customer, he hit the button. The mouse zipped out of the tub, over the glass, under the tables and straight into Steve's pocket.

'Vermin! Vermin!' screamed the woman climbing onto the nearest stool. It was like a scene out of *Tom and Jerry*, when Tom's owner, the maid, freaks out whenever she sees Jerry. I honestly thought she was going to faint with terror. Then the airport security staff charged onto the scene, some of them carrying machine guns, and the section was evacuated. It was chaos and a typical American overreaction. I'm surprised that flights in and out of Miami weren't cancelled for a few days. But I swear the woman was still standing on the stool screaming 'vermin' when we finally boarded our plane.

Let's face it, nobody likes airports, especially with all the new security procedures. But haven't we lost a bit of common sense along the way? Does it really f**king matter if the f**king plastic bag you've used for your toothpaste is two f**king inches too wide? Would it not be possible to use some common sense to decide that having the 'wrong'-sized plastic bag is not going to pose a threat to national security? Is it really worth sending me back to the end of the endless f**king queue for this reason? The only way these people get a job is by completing the question on the application form: Do you, in any circumstances where the smallest bit of common sense might be useful, ever use common sense? Y/N. If you answer 'No', the job's yours. Just how am I supposed to bring down an Airbus A380 with a tube of Sensodyne, anyway? And, by the way, the f**king tube doesn't fit in your smaller bags, so now I have to throw the whole thing away.

I probably shouldn't say this, but I'm going to. These jobsworths make you want to punch them on the chin. Of course, you should never do that. But that's how angry they make people feel and I'm sure a lot of people do lose their rag. Then security is called and you are banned from the flight – that's the reaction they want. If airports started treating passengers like humans, and not cattle, then the whole process could be stress-free and a lot quicker. I'm lucky because I am recognised quite a lot and get to jump the queues sometimes. But, coming back through Manchester Airport passport control, the queues are horrendous. Then you look to the next line along and anyone without a British passport is breezing straight through.

You may have guessed that I'm not a big fan of air travel. In fact, I try to avoid it whenever possible. Gone are the days when I would jump on a plane from Manchester to London, with just enough time to count to 10 before the cabin crew is preparing for landing. And driving isn't much of a better option.

It's impossible to plan any journey without hitting roadworks – exactly the same roadworks that were there last year, the year before that, and the year before that. And standing next to these exact same roadworks is the same labourer, eating exactly the same kind of butty he was eating three years ago and drinking his brew from the same mug. When they shout, 'Ey up, Foggy,' I'm tempted to shout back, 'Get back to work, you lazy bastard!'

Even when there are no roadworks – and, yes, this does occasionally happen – it's never easy. What happens, for instance, when a little bit of water starts to drop from the sky? Mayhem, that's what. It may have escaped many people's attention that the tyres on their cars are treaded. Therefore, it is perfectly safe to drive at the normal speed limit, assuming your windscreen wipers are working. But no, we all have to grip the wheel like we are clinging on to the Big Dipper at Blackpool Pleasure Beach and reduce our speed to 13.5 mph. And if it snows then the whole country grinds to a halt. Whenever the weatherman says, 'Don't go out unless you have to', I take that as a challenge and make up an excuse to go out and buy a loaf of bread. Sometimes I return, sometimes I don't – and then I have to ring Michaela to tell her I'm stuck. 'Idiot, you were warned not to go out. I'm not coming to get you, you'll have to leave the car and walk back,' is the usual answer.

It's not just the weather that can cause chaos. What, for example, might happen if I was to take my car on a narrow country lane? Then, halfway along that narrow country lane, another car comes towards me. Midway between our two cars is a very obvious widening of the road. You could even say the two cars could drive slowly past each other, the drivers could nod at each other as a way of agreeing that this was a job well done, and both cars could continue happily on their journey. Not on the lanes around my house! On these lanes, the approaching driver likes to ignore the wider points and drive right up to my face, as I wait patiently for them to realise that 'we are now f**king stuck, you stupid twat'. So, back up, and I don't care if you scrape your car along the stone wall in the process, and let's return to the point where two cars can pass each other quite easily. There. Simple. Have a nice day.

I now much prefer to take the train from Preston to London whenever I'm down there for meetings or TV stuff. I have to say that the full English breakfast in first class on Virgin Trains is awesome. (I also have to say that the fish and chips on the way back is shit.) I can be at Euston in two hours and 10 minutes from Preston on the fast trains, which is brilliant. Again, though, I'm lucky because someone else is normally picking up the cost of the ticket which at times can be embarrassing. For £450 one way, I would expect to be teleported to London. I bet Richard Branson has plans to do that soon. I'm afraid, though, that he won't be able to count on me as a customer on Virgin Galactic, his space travel company. I can't think of anything worse than being trapped in a spaceship so far away from the planet. You would have to *pay* me £100,000 to do that, never mind charging me that much. If people want that view so badly, what's wrong with Google Earth?

FOGGY PHENOMENA

10 foods and drinks
I couldn't live without

Cheese and Onion Lancashire crisps.

A cup of tea.

Vimto.

Meat and potato pie from Wild Flour Bakery, Blackburn.

KFC.

Fish and chips.

Full English brekkie on Virgin trains.

Crusty, salty burnt bit at end of Michaela's beef roast.

A nice cold beer in the summer – or winter, come to think of it.

Michaela's version of paella.

17

YOU CAN TAKE THE GIRL
OUT OF BLACKBURN . . .

You can't escape travel, especially when you live in the North West of England. It drives me nuts when it pisses down for days on end. I need to be outside, mucking around with the lads on bikes, riding my mountain bike or walking the dogs, not cooped up indoors. I honestly think the time of the year affects my mental health. I tend to suffer more from mood swings during the winter months and there is a recognised condition called Seasonal Affective Disorder. Some people call it Winter Depression and it's supposed to be due to lack of sunlight during those months. There's an easy cure for me – to brave the airports and the flights and to escape to somewhere nice and warm.

We used to have a holiday home in Spain and I'd like to have another one someday, somewhere. I'm a down-to-earth working-class British guy, so Spain would probably be the obvious choice again, possibly one of the Balearic Islands. Tenerife would be another possibility, although that's probably a little too far away. I love Italy but think I would feel a bit isolated there because of the language barrier. Even worse, I once thought I might have to spend the rest of my days in the middle of Germany.

I was appearing at a crazy event called Glemseck 100, near Stuttgart, as part of my ambassador role for Triumph. Glemseck is a rough-and-ready sprint festival full of beer-swilling Germans in dirty denim jackets, and I was competing on a souped-up Thruxton R in the Essenza Sprint. When the draw for the first round was announced, my arse nearly fell out.

'And riding against ze world superbike champion Carl Fogarty is ze top woman rider, Maria Costello,' shouted the announcer. I had no idea she was even at the event, never mind up against me in the first round. I've known Maria a long time, she's a great girl and I have a lot of time for her. And there's no doubt she can ride a motorbike. She's got something like eight silver replica trophies at the TT and has been third in support classes at the Manx Grand Prix and the North West 200. So I've got a lot of respect for her. But, if I had lost this sprint race, it would have been the end of my life as I knew it. Showing my face back in Britain would not have been an option. I was fully prepared to use all my spare euros to put down a deposit on a house in the nearest German village, grow some cabbages on a small plot of land, maybe keep a couple of pigs and see out my existence eating sausage and sauerkraut.

When I saw that she was on a trick BMW, my head went completely. Luckily, a practice run was scheduled, and I thought it would be a good idea to let her take the lead to see whether I would be able to recover. Sure enough, I was able to catch her quite easily. That was a bit of a relief, but I was still panicking. Anything could go wrong for the actual race. This time, when the girl dropped her neckerchief to signal the start, I went flat out and sneaked a glance across and saw that Maria was comfortably behind. Panic over. I was in the next round. And the next, and the next, and I ended up winning the final against another woman on a trick Kawasaki, who hadn't been beaten for a long time. Triumph Germany were pretty chuffed, and I gave the trophy to one of the lads who had come over from the Triumph factory in England.

My next sprint appearance didn't quite go to plan, though. This time it was for the launch of the Triumph Bobber at a warehouse in London, and Triumph had assembled an all-star team of me, Freddie Spencer and the girl from the Glemseck final, to take on the world's journalists. During the practice runs, we all realised that on the polished concrete floor it was pot luck whether you were going to get enough traction to win over such a short course. In the first round, I was up against a Brazilian journalist and made the fatal mistake of almost jump starting, so I ended up hesitating at the last fraction of a second. The journalist shot off and I knew immediately that I'd lost. How embarrassing – most people had assumed I was going to win the event hands down, including me. Never mind, Freddie will do us proud, I thought. Then he lost, too, and then the German girl. So, none of the all-star team made the semi-finals and Adam Child from *Motor Cycle News* ended up winning.

Maria has been a great ambassador for women riders, but I can't understand why she has always insisted that women should race against men professionally. It doesn't happen in any other motorsport. Women racers are at the same disadvantage as women tennis players, golfers or footballers – they can't be expected to have the same strength or speed of men. And that makes a big difference when racing the bigger bikes. One or two women have done okay in the smaller classes. Katja Poensgen scored points in a 250cc race, for example. But when it comes to super-bikes, I'd rather see the likes of Jenny Tinmouth racing against other women and winning, instead of coming nowhere against the men. People argue that there aren't enough women around to make a series. But everything has to start somewhere. If there are five riders in the first year, there might be 10 the following year and 20 in a few years' time.

Just because women aren't as strong doesn't make their sports any less enjoyable. I much prefer watching women's tennis, because the rallies are much longer. Give me a hot, sweaty Maria Sharapova match any day over an Andy Murray five-setter, even though he's Britain's best tennis player. (He's Scotland's best player when he's losing.) She's made more money than him, too. Her wealth is estimated at $125 million, while Murray's is $100 million. I'm not saying that's fair, it's just the way of the world. You are never going to get fat, buck-toothed girls with specs doing adverts for cosmetics. And I've never been offered modelling contracts, because I'm no David Beckham. (I'm not bad looking, though, am I?)

When women do compete against each other, that's when legends are made. Take the Spanish rider, Laia Sanz. She has been women's world tri-als champion around 13 times, has won the world enduro title for women and won the women's class at the Dakar. That's some going. Then there's Kiara Fontanesi, the Italian MX rider who has won the women's title five times. So, if women compete against each other in motocross and trials and enduro, why not in road racing? It doesn't make any sense. Maria makes a big point about running women-only track days, too. Doesn't that go against everything she is trying to achieve? Wouldn't a well-promoted, televised women's series not encourage more female riders on the roads?

Michaela enjoys riding a bike, although she sometimes lacks a bit of confidence. But when, in 2006, we were offered the chance to ride around New Zealand, she was really up for it. It was suggested to us by a guy called Adam Lacey, whose company Lace International produced all the successful *Hell for Leather* DVDs. The idea was for us to throw ourselves into all the crazy and beautiful stuff that the country has to offer, and the DVD would be called *Phileas Foggy's New Zealand Adventure*, after the guy in the book *Around the World in Eighty Days*.

The schedule was going to be tough, especially for Michaela on the big touring bikes that BMW were providing. She'd only passed her test in 2001, when she was working with the British bike manufacturer CCM, which we invested some money in – disastrously, as it turned out. But it's really good to see my mate, Austin Clews, whose family has owned and run CCM for a long time, doing well with the brand now. I always thought their market should be café racer-style bikes, and the new Spitfire they launched last year is a really cool bike. Michaela was shitting herself before she took her test and wore the green lucky vest that was cut from me after the crash at Phillip Island. But she passed at the first time of asking, although she described the pressure as 'worse than giving birth'. That was on a 500cc but she hadn't ridden anything bigger since then, so she needed a bit of practice on these bigger bikes.

The trip to New Zealand was going to be the longest time we'd ever been away from the kids, and it was really emotional saying goodbye. As soon as we landed, the cameras were in our faces 24/7 and it took some time for me to start being myself. When I did finally relax, it was probably the most amazing trip of our lives. We could speak to each other through mikes in our helmets, so the crew was always recording what was going on between us. We covered a lot of miles each day and the riding was a bit boring at times, so I'd try to entertain everyone with a song.

This was a bit like the party Michaela organised at home to celebrate my 50th and Claudia's 21st birthdays. We hired a massive tepee and had open fire pits, a photo booth, a tribute band and a cocktail van. And those cocktails were probably the reason that the only thing I remember was being up on stage with the band singing 'Wonderwall' by Oasis. I sounded mint, or so I thought. It wasn't until one of the lads who'd videoed my performance sent me the clip via WhatsApp the next day that the hideous truth was revealed. It was embarrassing. I'm not even sure it would possible to sing so out-of-tune if I tried. It's the sign of a good party, though, when the local constabulary pays at least a couple of visits.

Strangely, Michaela didn't appreciate my singing attempts in New Zealand, either. And she wasn't too keen when, if the ride was a bit uneventful, I would suddenly scream into my mike to watch her jump out of her skin. I think one of the best reactions was: 'Do that again and I'll f**king twat you!' It was slow going at times, especially when she refused to overtake any trucks, even though there was clear, straight road for the next 37 km. The lads in the support vehicle were pissing themselves when I stood on the pegs, flapping my arms and squawking like a chicken. Or I would do a running commentary: 'Michaela is thinking about overtaking the truck. I repeat, Michaela is thinking about overtaking. She is indicating to overtake.

And she is pulling out. She is now overtaking the truck. Michaela, has overtaken the truck. Repeat, Michaela has overtaken the truck. Woohoo!'

The other thing that kept us entertained, at least at the start, was my manager, Neil, driving the campervan containing all the back-up equipment. Bear in mind he's hopeless at driving anything bigger than a Mini. So this was a recipe for disaster. He scraped the van coming out of the hotel car park on the first day and it went downhill from there. He nearly took down the garden wall of one of the guesthouses we stayed in at Rotorua, a hot springs town that permanently stinks of rotten eggs, while attempting to reverse out of the drive. And he almost caused an inferno at a petrol station by ploughing into one of the pumps by completely failing to realise that the camper needed a slightly wider turning circle. After a while it wasn't funny, just annoying, and when he returned the van to the rental place the girl behind the counter nearly burst into tears when she saw the heap of scrap metal that remained.

Some of the challenges were more fun than others. For instance, we went diving with seals in Shark Bay, near Kaikoura, an amazing place on the South Island. Not happy. Seals have got to be top of the shopping list for sharks and it didn't help that the day was overcast, so we couldn't see a thing underwater. Our only previous experience of diving was at the Great Barrier Reef, in swimming pool conditions. Here, we were out of our depth and, if I had seen a seal down there, I would have shat my wetsuit. Luckily, the seals took a day off. That was on St Patrick's Day and we had time to let our hair down that night in a bar in Kaikoura before heading off to Christchurch the next morning. Word got around that I was in town and within an hour just about every Ducati owner for 500 km seemed to have turned up. I've never spent so much time talking about Aaron Slight! But the place was rocking and, before long, Michaela was dancing on the tables to Blondie, as usual. I think we rolled home at about 5 am, just time for two hours' kip before we hit the road again. That day's activity was enduro-riding, which would have been a lot more fun if my head wasn't as sore as a penguin's bollocks.

The final stop was Queenstown, the activity capital of the Southern Hemisphere. Again, a lot of the stuff we were doing here was out of my comfort zone, including an incredible helicopter trip, although the scenery soon took my mind off everything. It's where *The Lord of the Rings* films were made and is just breathtaking. The blue colour of some of the lakes seemed unnatural. We first flew down to the beautiful Milford Sound fjord, had a stroll on a remote beach, and within minutes we were landing at the top of one of the highest mountains, right on the edge of a glacier with sheer drops. It didn't help when the pilot told us that a big chunk of the glacier had crumbled away just the previous week. I've never been happier to get back in a helicopter.

The next day I did the Canyon Swing, a kind of bungee jump where you step off a ledge and drop 100 metres into a gorge to your inevitable death. The wind whistles past your ears and, just when your head is about to splatter on the rocks below, the wires swing you back up and across the gorge. The worst bit was being hauled back to the top – I was scrambling around like a maniac to try and get my feet back on solid ground.

That was my limit and I'd already told everyone that I didn't fancy skydiving later that afternoon. But Michaela had always wanted to jump from a plane – and there have been times I wanted to push her out of one. Only kidding, love you! Rohan Browning, the producer, was keen to film her, and to have a go himself. It was a beautiful, sunny afternoon, but really windy, and it was touch and go whether the people in charge were going to let them go up. I was waiting down on the ground and it had been agreed that Rohan would go first, then Michaela. It seemed to take ages before his parachute appeared but then, when he was about 20 metres from the ground, a gust of wind lifted him and the instructor back up for a second, then slapped them down on the ground. Rohan stuck his legs out to break the fall and crumpled in a heap. As you know, my immediate reaction is to laugh at someone else's misfortune, but I could quickly tell he'd hurt himself. By now, Michaela was on her way down and I was more concerned that the same thing might happen to her. She could hear Rohan's screams of agony from up in the air and knew something serious had happened but managed to stay focused and land without any problems.

Rohan went straight to hospital and the X-ray revealed that his ankle had basically shattered. There was nothing they could do except plaster it up and, fair play to him, he made it out for our wrap party that night in Queenstown. The next day, before we headed home, Michaela insisted on squeezing in one final dangerous activity – chucking her guts up in the middle of the main road, with massive logging trucks thundering past and honking their horns at her in appreciation. 'F**k off,' she growled back, mid-chunder. Goodbye, New Zealand, we will always keep a place for you in our hearts. And you will always have a piece of Michaela's stomach.

That trip was probably the launching pad for a few other adventures in the great outdoors, including a trek across Iceland for the NSPCC in 2016. I have been involved with the NSPCC for more than a decade. When I was thinking of somewhere to focus our charity efforts, the care of children seemed an obvious cause, because our two girls were in their teens at that time. I just couldn't stand the thought of anyone being cruel to a child, and some of the stories you hear make you feel physically sick. So, when Rachel Walker from the NSPCC came up to our house to tell us about an expedition they wanted me and Michaela to take part in, I was all ears and assumed it would involve bikes. When she told me about an Iceland trek, I thought she wanted me to do a sponsored walk to our local frozen food store (I wouldn't have been the first *I'm a Celebrity* winner to have an association with Iceland). But their idea was for people to raise enough money to come along on a four-day trek across the country during the summer, when the sun never sets. When Jake heard about it he was keen too, so the plan was changed to have two teams, Team Foggy and Team Jake. The places were filled almost straightaway, leaving me to fret for months whether my bad knee and ankle would stand up to that kind of punishment. I'd just had another operation on my knee and was struggling to walk two miles with the dogs, never mind 10 miles a day for four days.

It was another amazing experience. At the end of each day, we had to put up our tent and then someone would find a bottle of wine from somewhere, while the chef cooked stew. Various other expeditions also used these bases, and the only downside was the queue for the showers. It stretched all the way around the building. 'F**k this,' I thought, and just walked to the front, stripped down to my undies and washed myself under a tap in water that felt like a thousand knives stabbing me at the same time. 'Who is zees English idiot,' thought the rest of the Europeans.

Others thanked me for keeping my undies on. Michaela couldn't believe I'd done it, and I couldn't believe she didn't have a shower for three days.

Each night there was a team challenge, such as rolling Maltesers down a metal tape measure into your mouth. On the last night, it was the eating challenge. The score was one-all after the first two challenges, but there was only ever going to be one winner of this. After all, I had form. The dishes were all Icelandic national delicacies and a bit different to the jungle bush tucker. First up was sheep's head – straight down, no-brainer. Then sour ram's testicles, or súrir hrútspungar – a bit of a mouthful, but much better than mealworm. And finally, the national dish – fermented shark. How this can be the national dish of any country, I will never know. Thank f**k we have steak pie, chips, peas and gravy as our national dish. It stank of rotten fish, which was not surprising because it had been hung to dry for four months. But down it went, and my team were the winners.

I enjoyed chatting to the members of our group, too. One lad from Northern Ireland wanted to talk about the North West 200 constantly. He always wanted to turn everything into a challenge. 'I'll race you up there,' or 'I bet you can't lift that rock.' Then we came to a wide stream and it was a real pain to keep taking your boots and socks off to cross in the freezing cold water. So this lad says: 'I bet you can't jump across there, Carl, to be sure.' I looked at it and thought: 'I reckon I can just make it to the other side.' I went first, took a run-up and just about made it to the other side. Then it was his turn but, as he started his run-up, he stumbled halfway along and instead of stopping and starting again, he tried to carry on as if nothing had happened. But the weight of his rucksack meant he had too much downward momentum and, instead of launching off the bank, he went down like a sack of shit and face-planted straight in the water. 'Wah-hhhh!' I couldn't breathe for laughing. But I looked around and nobody else was joining in. 'Why do other people not find it as funny as I do when someone trips and falls?' I wondered. 'F**kin' hell, Carl. It wasn't that funny,' he grumbled, as he dragged himself back onto the bank. Actually, it was. I couldn't stop giggling for the rest of that day's trek. I didn't hear much from him after that.

The whole expedition raised more than £100,000 for the NSPCC and they were really chuffed, so much so that we are doing another in 2018. This time it's to Patagonia in Argentina for around 10 days. Anyone who's into hiking will tell you it's the place to go. You only have to Google the place to see why. But Michaela also has this idea of doing Everest Base Camp one day. She's on her own for that one – I'm pretty sure my knee and ankle wouldn't manage that. I wouldn't mind being helicoptered up there and mountain biking down, though.

FOGGY PHENOMENA
10 places

New Zealand

Amazing country, especially on bikes.

Tenerife

Blackpool with sunshine and a clean sea. Love it.

Barbados

Cool, mon.

Iceland

Probably prefer it in the summer!

La Villa, Dolomites

Favourite skiing resort.

Isle of Man

My spiritual home.

Northern Ireland

The people are so welcoming.

Ibiza

Great place for a party, but also a beautiful place to relax.

Anglesey

Great spot for me and Michaela to escape everything.

Home

18

I RECOGNISE YOU . . .

One of the things that *I'm a Celebrity* taught me about myself is that I'm much more confident being around strangers than I ever thought I could be. It was the same with that trip to Iceland. I didn't expect it to be easy to spend such long periods of time with people that I didn't know. I think my anxiety around new people was often seen as rudeness, but now I'm much more comfortable about being recognised and approached wherever I go. It can be useful, too.

I went to watch Oasis at the Royal Court Theatre in Liverpool with Michaela and a few mates in 2001. There was no VIP area, just a public bar, and I was being hassled to death. Then we spotted an area that was curtained off, so we snuck in to get out of the way. It turned out to be one of the private boxes, somewhere that the Royal Family might sit. And Scousers don't really like it if they think you are showing off. I'm not sure whether the gentlemen below us recognised me, but they started to make it quite clear they didn't like us looking down on them. One of them pointed at me and drew his finger across his throat. Perhaps he remembered that I was a Manchester United supporter! But in that situation, you don't hang around to try and make friends, so we headed back into the public bar. When we found our proper seats, we had to stand up to let a couple of guys past when the gig was due to start. They were both wearing those wigs and stick-on moustaches from Harry Enfield's 'calm down, calm down' Scouser characters, who are always getting into fights. For a laugh, I grabbed the first bloke's wig as he shuffled in front of me.

'Oh, f**k. It's his real hair.'

He turned around ready to land one on me but, luckily, recognised me and sort of laughed it off. Then, on the way back to the car park after the show, I was busting for a piss and had to go up against a wall. Next thing I knew, a hand grabbed the back of my shirt, dragged me away from the wall, mid-piss, and threw me in the back of a police van.

'You dirty bastard, get in there,' he shouted.

'Michaela! Get me out of here,' I yelled.

Everyone else in the van looked like they had just done 10 rounds with Mike Tyson. There was blood everywhere and it stank of booze. I thought I was going to be sharing a cell with these characters for days. Another copper then poked his head round the van door to tell me to stop shouting. 'For f**k's sake, it's you, Foggy, you stupid bastard. Get out, but next time we'll have to nick you,' he grinned. As I jumped out the other side, a couple more lads were thrown in. I think they just needed the space.

There was another time, when I was driving home from the race team unit in Burton and there had been an accident on the M6. The traffic was bumper to bumper and I quickly lost patience, so started nipping from one lane to another. Every time I changed lane, a black Mercedes followed me. Kev was with me and looked back to see that there were four big lads in the car. Then they started waving at us and pipping the horn. 'Shit, you've really pissed off this lot,' said Kev. 'Try and lose them.' There was a service station up ahead and I darted from the outside lane straight up the slip road. The black Merc did the same. I flew straight through the services and spotted a tiny gap to swerve back onto the motorway. 'I reckon you've lost them, you nutter,' said Kev, just as the black Merc pulled alongside us on the hard shoulder. I nearly shat myself. One of the lads was leaning out the back window and waving his arms at us to slow down. 'You'd better see what he wants,' I said to Kev, and I slowed right down.

'Can you pass this to Foggy to sign,' the guy said, and handed Kev a copy of my autobiography and a pen. 'We spotted your number plate miles back, but we couldn't keep up. You drive a car like you raced a bike,' he laughed. So had he been carrying that book around in his car on the off-chance that he might spot me on the motorway one day? Unbelievable. My first personal number plate, A8 FOG, cost me around £400. It was for my Mercedes Cosworth and I wanted people to think it was newer than it actually was. I've had them ever since, although there were times when I hated sitting in a traffic jam with everyone pulling funny faces and trying to catch my attention. I don't mind all that stuff now.

Another time that I was recognised, but perhaps wished I hadn't been, was when I was invited to Downing Street just after Tony Blair was elected. The event was held to launch a new government sports initiative and all the big names were there: David Beckham, Lennox Lewis, Ian

Wright . . . and James Whitham. 'What the f**k are you doing here? It's for famous sports stars,' I laughed. We weren't the only bike racers there, though, as the world speedway champion Gary Havelock turned up in a suit with a Diamante eagle on the back. Very weird. Before the official bit started, the waiters kept offering us canapés and champagne. It might be a Northern thing, or a motorbike thing, but when there's free grub and free booze, you fill your boots. I soon realised that I'd had a few too many, and I could tell that James was well on his way to being w**kered, too.

Eventually the sports minister, Chris Smith, started to introduce Tony Blair to all the guests. 'This is Carl Fogarty, Prime Minister – the world superbike champion.'

'Yes, I'm well aware of Foggy's achievements,' said Blair. 'I've always thought it would be good to go on a long bike trip one day with Cherie.' I was now aware that James had wobbled over to us and was listening in.

'You want to get yourself down to Benidorm on t' bike, Tony,' he slurred. Benidorm? Really? Where the f**k did that come from? You might have said the South of France, or the Amalfi Coast. But Benidorm? I laughed nervously and tried to nudge James out of the way. Then he dropped the most disgusting fart ever. The whole room heard him. Blair could obviously smell it and was obviously thinking: 'Who is this dirty bastard?' But he smiled politely and quickly moved on to the other side of the room. James tried to blame it on the nearest security guard: 'You can't drop your guts in front of the Prime Minster like that. Have you no shame, man?'

When it was time to go, we stumbled across Gary Havelock, who was worse for wear and curled up in a fireplace having a kip. Next I heard, he had been escorted out the back door of Downing Street to his van, which was parked in one of the side streets and had been clamped. He might still be there, for all I know. It's probably safe to say, though, that it will be a while before the bike-racing community will be allowed back inside Number 10.

It's one thing being recognised, but another thing completely to have a stalker. And mine is Emily, the most hideous female you have ever seen. She always wears an I ♥ Foggy T-shirt and her make-up and lipstick make her look even scarier. I first met her when I got back to my room in Spain after a few beers with the lads who go enduro-riding with a company called Torotrail. I pulled back the duvet and this dwarf-sized doll was lying in my bed in a nurse's uniform, staring at me like a crazy woman. I nearly jumped out of my skin and I could hear them all giggling in the corridor. And, the more something annoys me and winds me up, the more they will go out of their way to do it. So Emily hides in my wardrobe, suitcase (without legs) on top of the door, so that when I come to leave my room in the morning it falls on my head. They get me with it every time. Lyndon, who runs Torotrail, even flew her over to England to sit at the top of the table at a curry house after a day's riding. It's really quite sad when you have to go to such lengths to keep yourselves amused.

This bunch of mates has got me into trials bikes recently, and that's something I never thought I would say. My first go was a complete disaster, at an event called Shark X-Treme for Shark helmets. This was two days of tough riding and sleeping under a bivouac in the foothills of the Pyrenees and there were some decent riders taking part. Just one problem – it was an enduro event, not trials. So when they asked me what bike I wanted to ride, I told them any decent trail bike. But they thought I meant trial bike. So, while everyone else was on trick KTMs, I'm on a f**king Sherco. 'We thought it was a strange choice,' they said. I was knackered after an hour and the organisers were already packing up by the time I arrived at the various checkpoints. Then I fell off on a rocky section and cut my knee. There was a doctor on hand, or someone who had once seen the French version of *Casualty* on TV, and he rubbed this weird-smelling ointment around the cut. I reckon he was actually just having a laugh with his French mates: 'Let's try zees horseshit cream on ze knee of Foggy. Oui?' An hour later and my knee was the size of a balloon from an allergic reaction and I obviously had to pull out. The upside was that I made it back in plenty of time for a party at our house. James took me to hospital early the next morning – and he's not one to make a drama out of a medical situation.

I always used to say trials was like ballet dancing on a bike. But I have massive respect for Dougie Lampkin, who I know well and has something like 16 world titles – indoor, outdoor and team championships – to his name. To completely dominate a sport for so long is amazing and what he can do on a bike is off the scale. The *Sunday Times* newspaper once set up a feature on Dougie teaching me how to ride for a day. I wasn't doing too badly, until he advised me not to try one very steep bank. Red rag time again ... Towards the end of the day, I pulled up to the bank and looked across to see Dougie shaking his head. I could tell exactly what he was thinking: 'The dickhead's going to have a go. Don't do it.' And I almost made it to the top – almost. Instead, I flipped it right at the top of the banking and went arse over tit all the way down, with just one broken finger to show for it. This was just a few days before the Goodwood Festival of Speed, where Dougie was booked to ride through Goodwood House, the home of Lord March. So he's basically riding a bike through the corridors of a stately home and even disappeared out of one of the bedroom windows at one stage. Anyone who hadn't seen trials before thought he was some kind of illusionist, like David Blaine, and not a motorbike rider.

Trials is a good substitute for motocrossing, which is more dependent on the weather and there aren't too many tracks near where I live. I'm actually loving my new Sherco trials bike and even had a lesson recently at Inch Perfect in Clitheroe. I'm not normally a good listener, but I paid attention on this occasion and picked up tips on the importance of correct position on the bike, keeping momentum, and not spinning the wheels on a rock face. Their lads were waiting to catch you if you don't quite make it. I was pumped – and was doing really well until the log-balancing stuff. I couldn't work out how to get the front wheel up on the log, and then the back wheel without smashing the engine casing into the log, although I did finally get the hang of it. The ones who weren't as good on the other sections did it first time, much to everyone's amusement.

But you can't beat an enduro ride-out. Again, I'm usually first to have a go whenever we come to a gnarly, rocky bit. Lyndon will tell me to stay in second and take it steady, but I'm like a bull in a china shop when, instead, a bit of finesse and throttle control is needed. And when I don't make it at the first attempt, the other lads will be desperate to do better, just so they can rub it in.

One of the lads, Warren Cooper, used to be a decent motocross rider and came on one of our enduro rides for the first time on another wet day in the Lake District. I was a long way ahead with the guy who was leading the ride, Andy, and we came to a river crossing, but it was too deep and the current too strong to cross. Andy went first but rode down the side of the river until he found a section that was rockier, and just about made it across. I followed him the same way and then we both rode up the opposite side of the bank and back to the crossing. When Wozza arrived, it looked like we had gone straight across the crossing. Wozza stopped and I could see he was thinking: 'How the hell am I going to get across there?' So he nodded to me, wanting reassurance that it was okay to cross there. I gave him the thumbs up and off he went. Down and down. I'd actually thought the water would only reach the engine casing. But soon all you could see was the top of his helmet. And a few bubbles coming from below the surface. I had no idea it was going to be that deep.

'You f**king bastard,' he gurgled. 'You'd better go and get a van to drag this out right now.' He couldn't splutter his words out he was so angry. You can always get a two-stroke running again in 20 minutes by turning it upside down, taking the plug out and drying it, then kicking it over a few times. But it took a lot longer than usual, because I couldn't stop laughing that I'd stitched him up big time. And that's what it's all about – a few mates, a few belly laughs (even if it's at my expense) and a few beers. Just not with Emily around . . .

19

FAINTING GOATS

The Fogarty household has always been filled with animals. And I'd be the first to admit we haven't always got it right with pets. The current bunch are Desmo, Beano, and Storm. Desmo, short for Desmosedici, the Ducati engine, is a handsome boy, a Red Fox Labrador who doesn't like people who do not live with him. He's fine with Michaela but doesn't respect me as an authority figure. If I tell him off for any reason, he growls at me even more. Then there's Beano, a Jack Russell, who doesn't like people who do not live with him. He's fine with Michaela but doesn't respect me as an authority figure. If I tell him off for any reason, he growls at me even more. Can you see the pattern? I must have annoyed them both as puppies, so I have tried to do things differently with Storm, a Blue Staffy, who was a present for Claudia's 23rd birthday.

When I was growing up, if a dog did something wrong Dad would give it a whack on the nose with a rolled-up newspaper. Now the advice is to reward good behaviour. If the puppy shits in the house, I pick it up gently and carry it into the garden and tell her nicely where she should be shitting. If she does something right, I reward her with a treat. Hopefully she might not turn out like the other two – we wait with bated breath. Because when anyone turns up at our house, all hell breaks loose. Visitors have to be very brave to venture through the front door with Desmo and Beano yapping at their heels.

Beano was a replacement for another Jack Russell, Keano, named after the footballer, Roy Keane – and the story of Keano is really sad. It was a hot day in 2007, just before I went over to the TT for the centenary celebrations. Michaela was training in our gym with her personal trainer and Kev came round with a twin-axle trailer on his car to drop a couple of bikes off. As he was pulling away down the drive, I could see the straps flapping around. I shouted for him to stop and I ran down the drive to tie the straps together. Keano ran with me and, just as I told Kev that it was okay to go, the dog darted under the trailer. I yelled at him to stay where he was and, if he'd done that, he would have been okay. But he tried to escape between the two sets of wheels and the back set ran straight over him. How was I going to tell Michaela that her dog was dead? First, I had to pick it off the drive and put it in the field, so that she wouldn't see it. Then I went into the gym, just looked at Michaela and she knew something was seriously wrong.

'What's happened?' she cried.

'Keano's dead. It wasn't his fault, but Kev ran over him,' I told her.

It was a horrible day. Michaela was in floods of tears all day, Kev didn't know what to do with himself, and then I had to pick the kids up from school and tell them what had happened. They both cried their eyes out. We were all in bits for days. Then somebody told us to get another dog straightaway, and that's the best advice anyone has ever given me. We wanted another Parson Jack Russell, found a breeder with puppies for sale and Kev paid for Beano, to try and put things right. And Beano has hated me ever since.

Also at the house I have a big cock, obviously, and some chickens. I also want some ducks and a turkey. At least turkeys talk back to you. It would possibly be the most meaningful conversation I've had with a bird. (Did you see how I mentioned turkeys there without making a joke about gobbling?) I also want to try pigs again. We used to have two Vietnamese pot-bellied pigs called Scott and Aaron, after my rivals Scott Russell and Aaron Slight. That all got out of hand, though, when the neighbours' pig escaped and shagged ours, which were actually female, despite their names. Suddenly, we had about 12 of these piglets, which looked like giant rats, creating mayhem everywhere. They once all escaped into our five-acre field and, from the hideous sound of them squealing their heads off as we tried to round them up, the neighbours probably thought we were torturing them. It took about four hours to catch them all. So they had to go. If I had another pig, I think I'd call it Jimmy, because of the amount of squealing Jimmy Bullard did in the jungle.

But the thing that I really, really want are some fainting goats. I reckon even we can't go wrong with fainting goats. You can do what you want to them. They just keel over and pretend to be dead. Every time I fire up one of my bikes, the whole field will just topple to the ground. And I can't think of anything funnier than creeping up behind them with an air horn.

The chickens could have been a disaster with Beano and Desmo around. It didn't start well when Beano grabbed one on their first day outside the coop. All that was left was the beak, the cord running through the head and bits of the wings. So I belted him on the nose and tied what was left of the chicken around his neck and let him wander round in shame for a few hours. It seemed to do the trick because none of the dogs have bothered the chickens since. Storm chased them a bit at first, but we carried her away and rewarded her when she left them alone, and I think she has learnt from the other two not to bother them. The chickens are good layers, but there's only me that will eat their eggs. Michaela and the girls won't touch anything that has come fresh out of our own chickens' bums and insist on Marks & Spencer's eggs instead. So, every morning, I write the date on the eggs and have about three, scrambled on toast for breakfast, which I make for myself, thank you very much.

Okay, I may not be *MasterChef* material, but I reckon I'm pretty good at the basics. I can do a mean steak on the barbie, with a few boiled potatoes and salad. It's when we get to things like sauces that I come a bit unstuck, although you can't go wrong with Bisto. I have been asked to go on *Celebrity MasterChef* a couple of times, but it's not for me. I reckon those two pompous p***ks would be wearing my dishes if they criticised my presentation. I'm not a fan of cookery programmes at all. Michaela watches every one, so I'm surprised her cooking hasn't improved. Just kidding. She's an excellent cook – and the burnt, salty bit at the end of her Sunday roast beef is my favourite food on earth. But chefs seem to think they are so superior, although there are a few decent ones. Paul Hollywood from *Ready Steady Bake-off*, or whatever it's called, is a good guy and is into his bikes. And I have met the Hairy Bikers a few times. Northern lads, who love their bikes and can make a decent pie – what's not to like? And I used to enjoy watching Hugh Fearnley-Whittingstall foraging around in the show *River Cottage* and cooking up squirrel stew.

I'd be good at foraging. I'd definitely be one of the survivors if there was ever a nuclear holocaust. I'd have the best shelter on the planet and I'd be happy catching squirrels to cook them on a camp fire. In fact, if we'd been able to hunt for own food, I'd have been happy to stay in the jungle. My basic instincts aren't that far removed from the Neanderthal. These days, I definitely wouldn't get away with beating a woman over the head and then having sex with her, but maybe there's still a bit of caveman in me!

If I was to compare myself to anyone, it would be Homer Simpson. It might be a bit worrying that I relate so well to this cartoon yellow blob. But he tries to simplify life, as I do. He says it like it is, occasionally puts his foot in it and his brain often lets him down. I've learnt a lot from Homer – mainly not to pay too much attention to the consequences of my actions.

If there's no decent sport on the telly, and no Simpsons, I'll flick through the channels to find something that teaches me about real life, like a wildlife documentary or even a Bear Grylls show. This stuff is way better than the *Real Desperate Housewives of Cheshire* and all that other reality and soap shit that's on throughout the rest of the house.

The one thing I definitely won't watch is *News at Ten*. Who the f**k wants to hear about war and murders and rapes and terrorism just before they go to bed? I can just about stomach it in the morning, because I can hopefully forget about it all by lunchtime. I'm no expert in world affairs, but religion seems to be the cause of some of these problems. Personally, I don't believe in life after death. Hopefully I'm proved wrong, and I float up to find a pool party at Elvis' house, with cold beer on tap and a couple of dirt bikes and jet-skis to muck around on. That would be a bonus. Wahoo! But if there is an afterlife, then I might be going somewhere very hot.

If that character Davy Jones from the *Pirates of the Caribbean* films asked me 'Do ye fear death?' the answer would be a loud 'no'. I think that's the same for most racers. They just can't afford to have that fear in the backs of their minds. But the most horrible thing I've ever had to witness was the slow death of my mum, Jean, two years ago.

My mum and dad split up in 1998 and Mum went to live with my sister, Georgina, in Lanzarote. When Mum came back to live in England in 2008, we knew something was not right. She was losing her memory, had problems moving her arms and was eventually diagnosed with a rare form of Alzheimer's. For her last two or three years, when she was in a home, she had absolutely no quality of life. She couldn't speak and showed no signs of recognising us. Her eyes just followed us blankly around the room. Her weight dropped to five stone yet, when someone offered her some mushed-up food, she just opened her mouth and accepted it. I was willing her to turn it down so that she could be out of her misery. And it got me thinking that I'd like to put something in place in case something similar happened to me. If someone gave me a form which said that, once everyone agreed I'd lost my faculties, I could be on the first plane to Switzerland, then I would sign it today. Michaela and the girls love me, so they would understand. I cannot understand any argument against euthanasia.

We all do it for our pets when they are too sick to carry on. We put them out of their pain and misery. Why can't we do that for humans?

Although I'm not scared of death, I'm usually the first in tears at a funeral, especially when the music comes on. For Mum we played 'You're So Vain' by Carly Simon, because she always took a lot of pride in her appearance. That year was a bad one for our family, because the girls' other grandma, Pat, Michaela's dad's wife, also died. At her funeral, we played the theme from *Titanic*, 'My Heart Will Go On' by Celine Dion. It was hard to lose both my mum and Pat in the space of 18 months, because they were such an integral part of our lives and played such a big part in raising the girls while we were away racing.

Then just last year, my Uncle Brian passed away. He was a loveable rogue, who I fell out with for around 14 years when there was a legal dispute over some of my merchandise rights. He basically fell in with the wrong crowd, but I had so much fun with him in the early days of my career in the early 1980s. Brian was there when I won my first world title, the TT Formula One title at Donington in 1988. When I dropped to my knees in the gravel after I won my fourth World Superbike title at Hockenheim, Brian was in front of me in the crowd. I met him for lunch shortly before he died and he told me that he was thinking of his mum, Vera, my grandma, when he saw that. Brian's funeral was quite emotional for me, especially when my dad, his two other brothers, Phillip and Jimmy, and one of my cousins, carried the coffin in to 'He Ain't Heavy, He's My Brother' by The Hollies. Then they played 'My Way'. There's no doubt Brian did it his way, rightly or wrongly.

Having said all that about religion, I'll admit that there were times when

I sat on the starting grid and thought: 'Look after me here, I might need a bit of help in this race.' Perhaps that's hypocritical, too, although I don't think I was thinking religiously. However, I was very superstitious and maybe I thought that fate could play a helping hand. So call it fate, call it what you will, but two of my early crashes certainly helped shape my career.

I was actually pretty scared of pain as a kid, ever since I split my head open running away from a bull. Okay, it might have been an angry cow, but bull sounds better. At the edge of the field, I had to jump over a stream to safety, but I didn't quite make it and smacked my skull on the opposite bank. (A bit like that Irish lad in Iceland, but this one wasn't funny.) Three or four nurses had to hold me down for the stitches. And I was terrified of needles after that – again I needed to be held down for my first tetanus jab before going to watch my dad in the Spanish GP, or whenever I went to the dentist.

My first bad crash was during practice for a 350cc race at Mallory Park in 1985, when I high-sided coming out of the Esses. I made the mistake of hanging on to the bike, and with the throttle wide open, so I hit the tyre wall hard and the impact threw me over the fence into the field. I came round covered in weeds and nettles near Devil's Elbow, and it was ages before the ambulance reached me because they took the wrong track initially. I was dazed and confused, and thought I'd won the Spanish GP. But it didn't take long to realise my arm was broken, and there was a big gash on the inside of my thigh, which must have caught the top of the fence. When the medic arrived, he could see I was concussed and asked: 'Do you know the name of the Prime Minister?' I think I answered Queen Elizabeth, or something daft.

The following year, I was making a name for myself in the British 250cc Championship. I'd just won the big race at Scarborough before finishing eleventh in the British GP. Then I went practising at Oulton Park, but only had a couple of old slicks that had been stuck in the garage for a few years. Not the smartest move I ever made. Coming out of a long sweeping bend at around 100 mph, I lost the rear and knew I was in trouble. When I looked down at my leg, I knew I was in *big* trouble. It was at a weird angle and I didn't even realise at that point that the femur had broken through the skin.

That was a long road to recovery. Nowadays it would have been plated but, back then, the doctors reset the bone and I had to lie on my back in hospital for eight weeks while weights held the bones in place. When I started to race again in 1987, it took a while to adjust to the movement I lost in the knee, but I was back to winning ways midway through the season. Then, at the Silverstone round of the British 250cc Championship, I slid off in the wet for the softest of crashes. James saw the crash from the pit-wall and this time he thought that I was being a soft twat. I remember calmly asking for gas and air . . . before starting to scream. Maybe I hadn't been taking the antibiotics that the doctors prescribed when the pin was removed after the initial break, but the bone had become infected and it was so weak that it had snapped easily. The bad bone was scraped out and the leg was put in an external fixator for ages.

That crash was on 19 September. The Mallory crash was on 19 May and Oulton on 19 August. Didn't I break my collarbone on my 19th birthday, too? Hang on a minute, there's something happening here. (And I've just realised that all this is in Chapter 19 . . .) If there had been a race on

19 October 1988, I just wouldn't have turned up. But those two bad leg breaks did make it harder for me to get comfortable on the smaller bikes. On superbikes it was a different story. The leg didn't give me half as much trouble. It was as though the decision to move up to bigger bikes, where I had all my success, was made for me.

Riders do tend to be a superstitious bunch. You want the odds stacked in your favour, so why not use every advantage that might be available? Apart from the number 19, the other number I tried to avoid was number 3. When I started out in schoolboy motocross, I always wanted to be number 3, so that I could be like the cool American rider, Gene Romero. Then I broke my leg twice, so switched to number 4. There was another funny coincidence much later, when I announced my retirement on 21 September 2000. Then, on very same date the following year, I broke my leg in that supermoto crash.

I was also superstitious in a positive way, though. I first started to wear something green at the North West 200 in 1993. I qualified on pole but, despite being fastest there for a number of years, I'd never managed to win for one reason or another. One of the locals said that I needed the Luck of the Irish and that I should find something green to wear. It just so happened that Michaela had a green Benetton vest with her, so I thought there was no harm in giving it a go. Sure enough, I won both races and set a new lap record.

I wore that green Benetton vest for 57 of my 59 world superbike wins. For one of those two other wins, at Sentul in Indonesia, we had packed it but left it at the team hotel, which was half an hour drive from the hotel. There was no time to go back, so my team manager, Virginio Ferrari, raced round to the local shopping centre, bought a greenish T-shirt and chopped the arms off to make it look like a vest. On the other occasion, I borrowed a green T-shirt from one of the Kawasaki teams. The original lucky green vest was finally cut from me after the crash that ended my career in Phillip Island. It brought me luck right up until the final moment of my career, because I'm still here today. We framed it after Pat, the kids' grandma, stitched it up, and it now has pride of place in my garage showroom.

FOGGY PHENOMENA
Bucket list

Diving with sharks.

Cresta Run.

European night at Anfield.

Catching salmon in Alaska.

Glastonbury – with access all areas pass. Any suggestions?

A doughnut on the 18th green at St Andrews on a motocross bike.

Singing on stage with Oasis.

Land's End to John o' Groats, off road on an enduro bike.

Going back in the jungle.

A table at The Brit Awards, somewhere near Liam and Noel.

20

BORN AGAIN

It would be cool to have been born in the 1950s instead of a decade later. As a teenager in the 1960s, I would have remembered England winning the World Cup. I would have seen more of George Best and Mike Hailwood in action. I would have grown up with The Beatles. I might even have been a hippy – along with Michaela, of course. I would have been able to drive fast cars without wearing a seat belt, and ride my bike as fast as I wanted to. Back then, motocross tracks were proper men's tracks, like the one at Namur in Belgium, with big, long, fast, sweeping bends where you could actually out-brake somebody. Now they are full of whoops and jumps and are a lot more technical. In the same way, some of the great fast circuits like Hockenheim, Zeltweg and Assen have all changed and lost their magic.

Don't get me wrong, the 1970s were still great for a kid. Everything just seemed better than it is now. Milk was delivered to our doorstep – full cream. There were no CCTV cameras when I nicked off school. Pop was delivered to our doorstep – full sugar. I could slather a load of butter on my bread without being tutted at. There were only three TV stations and the shows were much better. *Grange Hill*, for instance, or *Top of the Pops* (especially with Pan's People). I could play football with my mate on a main road, because there was no traffic. I could play conkers at school. Basically, you didn't have to worry about health and safety every time you so much as farted, or worry about being politically correct every time you opened your mouth. People lived, instead of just existing.

This isn't the worst time to be alive, either. I reckon I could pick a lot worse periods to be a human being in the six million years we've been on the planet. But, as every year goes by, the world gets crazier and crazier. Technology has a lot to answer for. It drives me mad to see kids sitting around staring at the telly or their phones. Go outside, build a treehouse, kick a ball around, ride a dirt bike or hide in the bushes and jump out and scare the shit out of somebody. Just do something.

We have become so dependent on technology that it's difficult to cope when it goes wrong. We recently had a lot of work done at our house and we now have a room that looks like the bridge of the Starship Enterprise – and that's just to control all the lights, underfloor heating and other security stuff. But I like to be the person who climbs onto a stool and changes the lightbulb. Now I have to call a team of computer geeks to come round. And the shit we had to go through when we wanted to switch internet providers was absolutely disgusting. There were times when Michaela was in tears trying to find the right person at Sky to give her an answer to what should have been a very simple question. The problem, of course, was that she was speaking to someone about 5,000 miles away in somewhere like India, who could barely speak our language and had no idea how to deal with our problem, except by providing infuriating answers from a manual. And that's before she was cut off and had to start the process all over again with a different person, probably in a different country. The man or woman who invented call centres is probably very wealthy now. But I want you to take a good hard look at yourself. Have you really made the world a better place? Then I want the people who make the decisions to set up call centres to take an even harder look at themselves. Do you realise the stress and anxiety and suffering you cause good honest people with these abominations – all in the name of profit and greed. The banks, electricity and gas providers, and phone and internet companies who set up call centres are supposed to deliver a service. But you often have to beg for help. It's criminal the way people are treated.

I do welcome technology when it can make a genuine difference, though. If that means improvements in safety without ruining the fun, all the better. That's why I recently became involved in a product called Zona. It's a camera system that's attached to the back of a bike which links wirelessly to a tiny screen which fits inside the rider's helmet. It basically works like a rear-view mirror. Without turning your head, you can glance at the screen for a fraction of a second and see everything that's happening behind you in amazing clarity. No more turning back and missing what's happening in front, which causes a lot of crashes. It can be adapted for other helmets, too, like cycling and skiing. I'm not saying it will ever replace side mirrors on motorbikes completely, but I'd be surprised if didn't become an essential piece of kit for every rider soon.

There are times when technology is just plain nuts. Driverless cars are bad enough. But riderless motorbikes? Give me a break. Apparently, it won't be long before they are available, and Honda unveiled a prototype at a show last year. This one is supposed to be safer in slow-moving traffic, or when the rider wants to relax. We all know riding a bike can be dangerous. I'm exhausted after a long ride because I focus so hard on trying to predict what everyone else might do on the road, especially car drivers. But when something happens, you need a human in the seat to react to the danger, not a computer. Sorry, Honda, but this has to stay as science fiction, in my lifetime at least.

I was once asked to star with Scarlett Johansson in a science fiction film featuring bikes, called *Under the Skin*. She played an alien who seduces Scottish men before eating them. I would have been her protector, who basically rides around on his bike disposing of the bodies and cleaning up after her. It would have been a non-speaking role and the casting director was looking for someone who could be 'at one with the bike', but at the same time be quite sinister looking. I can't imagine why they chose me. It would have meant about three weeks of filming in the wilds of Scotland and I wouldn't have had the patience for that. The money wasn't great, either. The only thing that did appeal was looking after Scarlett Johansson for three weeks. I turned it down and heard later that it was offered to Jeremy McWilliams.

I could always see myself playing the bad guy, a bit like Vinnie Jones. But the only time I've given acting a bit of a go was when I was approached to star in a Status Quo film – as myself. It would have been set in Thailand and I would have helped the Quo lads out of a few scrapes, with lots of motorbike stunts and chase scenes. The man behind the film, a guy called Stuart St Paul who had worked on Bond films, struggled to raise the money for that project, although he released a similar film about 10 years later called *Bula Quo*, filmed on Fiji. He insisted I had real potential though, so arranged to take me to the Leeds set of one of the shows he was working on at the time, *Emmerdale*, to have a look behind the scenes at how it all works. I went with Michaela and my manager, Neil, and they all persuaded me to try a very basic screen test. All I had to do was enter the set for the Woolpack pub and have a chat with the barman. But I just couldn't get my head around it. I wanted to say what I would have said in that situation, not the lines they were telling me to say. It didn't help that Michaela and Neil pissed themselves laughing every time I opened my mouth. I was getting annoyed and frustrated, so I only tried two or three takes. Even so, Stuart persisted and created a part for me in another of his film projects called *The Bogfather*. Yes, that's right, *The Bogfather*! It was about a bunch of gangsters who, on the surface, made their money providing outdoor toilets for big events, but who were really involved in trafficking women. Again, it was taking a long time to find the funding, so I eventually lost interest. But the film was finally released, again about 10 years later, with a new title, *Freight*. I wonder why they changed it.

I do know that if I'd ever given acting a go, or anything else for that matter, Michaela would have supported me 100 per cent. She has been there through thick and thin. People forget that we had a crush on each other when we were just kids, and that we first lived in a shitty one-bedroomed apartment in a rough area of Blackburn when I was starting out in racing. The success came much later, and I don't think it works the other way round – when you marry someone because they are successful. We've always been a team and I couldn't have done it without her. Any rider, or any sportsman for that matter, needs someone there when it's not going right. Someone who is willing to listen and offer an opinion. Michaela has always been a straight-talker, but she has always had that soft side, too. Nowadays, it's more of the straight-talking. 'You've left your shitty underpants on the floor again, you scruffy bastard. Go and pick them up.' Yes, miss.

Another important thing is that she's the life and soul of any party and has always got on well with my mates, even if some of them are scared stiff of her, with good reason. One time, Kev came round for a few glasses of wine and the three of us were watching a crap TV show about Brazilians – waxing, not the football team. Michaela asked Kev if he'd ever shaved his pubes and, when he said 'no', she suggested that we try out a new waxing product on him. Kev, of course, was up for anything. 'Go and get your cock in a sock,' she laughed and, when he came back in the room, Michaela poured a load of wax on him as he sat on the settee with his pants around his ankles and a disgusting, smelly Nike sock hiding his little acorn. 'It can't be as bad as having a football boot stud stuck into my shin,' said Kev, confidently. She put the first strip in place and pulled it off so hard that all the skin came off too. Kev went blind for a few seconds with the pain. Michaela was dancing around the room like an Apache warrior who'd just scalped John Wayne. 'Get an ambulance,' Kev whimpered, which wasn't a bad idea because I needed oxygen, too. I'm told he had to make up excuses for not having sex with his wife for six weeks.

Me and Michaela are lucky that we have the time to do lots of stuff together, like walking the dogs, or taking our bikes out for a ride in the summer for a pub lunch or dinner – she has a Triumph Street Cup. But obviously, after 25 years of marriage, we do have the occasional tiny disagreement. I might leave a cushion five inches out of place after she has been away for a night; or Michaela might want to go to Barbados for a holiday, but I want to go to Tenerife. What we want from a holiday is very different, too. Michaela is happy to chill on a sunbed with a good book, but I can't keep still for five minutes. I'm in and out of the sea all day – on jet-skis, water-skis or wakeboards. Then we might not always agree where we should go to eat in the evening. I'm happy with fried fish from one of the locals on the beach, which costs $2. Michaela prefers somewhere fancy like The Cliff, where the starters cost $200.

It's mainly Michaela who manages our finances, and she does a great job, but I'm definitely the bigger worrier about money. That's probably because I went out there and risked my life to earn it. I'm also from a working-class background and my dad was always careful with money. It's probably a Northern thing, too. You never know what's around the corner and when it all might end. It wouldn't bother me if it did. I'd probably go out and get a job as a truck driver. But I don't flash it around and I have no idea how much we're worth, I just know that we have invested wisely and have always had good advice from our financial adviser, Martin Williams. All I need to know is whether there's enough in the bank for a new dirt bike. And it's true that the more famous you are, the less you spend. People are willing to do a deal because of who you are or what you can bring to the table.

I'm better at remembering special occasions now, like Valentine's Day or wedding anniversaries. That wasn't always the case, but I have learnt the hard way that my life isn't worth living if I forget. I used to rely on Michaela's friend, Tracey, to help me with her Christmas shopping, but I'm better at all that now and I enjoy buying presents. That wasn't always the case. But, if there's one thing that does still annoy me, it's how much women spend on making themselves look beautiful – not just Michaela, the girls too. It's not just their hair, these days. It's nails, eyebrows, toenails and f**k knows what else that I don't get told about. I have my hair cut every eight weeks, not every two weeks. When my nails do need cutting, I do it with a pair of scissors. I don't need someone else to do it for me. And I have never once said: 'You're not coming out with me tonight, your toenails are too dirty.' If you find your toenails that offensive, I'll Tippex them for you – and it will take me five minutes, not two hours. I don't mind her taking pride in her appearance and buying new clothes when she needs them – not too much, mind. But I don't like having to fork out for all that other stuff. (It's the doghouse for me when she gets her hands on this book!)

When we do spend money, we try to spend it on something that's not going to go down in value. And we've now got the house looking awesome. It's got a view to die for and I can sit outside on the patio and stare out over the hills of the Ribble Valley, all the way over to Blackpool Tower. We can even see the Lake District on a good day. Yet I'm still a stone's throw from where I was born. I'm a Northern lad through and through, and proud of my roots. Yes, I have a very comfortable life and, yes, I have a lot be thankful for. But I have earned it and I have managed to keep my feet on the ground. And I have faced all the challenges and tragedies that life has presented. I think I'm a better person for that – a lot more likeable than Carl Fogarty, the racer. *I'm a Celebrity* played a big part in that change, and winning that show will always be a really proud moment in my life.

Most of all, though, I'm proud of my family – Michaela, Danielle and Claudia. Who knows, that family may grow one day. I haven't really thought about being a granddad. I would probably spoil them, for sure. I expect I would enjoy annoying them, too, especially the boys, like tripping them up when they are learning to walk, or taking them out in the field on a bike and telling them to see what happens when they twist that throttle back as far as they can.

But before the kids fly the nest for good and leave me and Michaela to rattle around this house, I have one final ambition. The technology in the new house allows us to operate everything from anywhere in the world from my mobile. So, the next time I'm bored on a beach in Barbados, I'm going to work out the time that Claudia has just fallen fast asleep. Then, on my phone, I'm going to open all the curtains, turn the heating on full blast, switch on all the lights except the one in her room – and then belt Oasis out of the loudspeakers at full volume. She will shit herself.

And that will be my proudest achievement of all.

ACKNOWLEDGEMENTS

Big shouts out for their help with this book to: Michaela; Kevin Moore; James Whitham; all the team at Headline, especially Jonathan Taylor; Tony Hudson; Austin Clews; Tom Whiting; Dave Daniels; Scott Smith; and last, and definitely f**king least, to Neil Bramwell, for harassing and stressing me throughout the whole process ☺.

PICTURE CREDITS

INDEX